"Packed with thoughtful insights accessible to any reader, Dr. William Varner has produced an invigorating handbook for these two Solomonic works that offers refreshing strategies based on internal features of the text. By surveying their 'big picture,' Varner applies a top-down method of discourse analysis that views the entire text as a literary unit rather than the sum of individual verses. What emerges are internal literary structures that brilliantly suggest three intermingling characters engaged in the dramatic love story of the Song and a two-part interpretive frame for Kohelet following the text's 'goads' and 'nails' arrangement. The Preacher and the Song offers an engaging and readable volume that exalts the divine beauty and theology of these two ancient masterpieces."

**Cory Marsh, Ph.D.**
Professor of New Testament
Southern California Seminary

"With his gift for making deep insights easy to grasp, Dr. Varner grounds Solomon's writings in his personal journey. Joined with careful attention to context, the result emphasizes the constructive message in Ecclesiastes as well as an interpretation of The Song of Songs that seeks to do justice both to its details and the formative choices in the life of Solomon–the wayward cum chastened king."

**Brian Morley, Ph.D.**
Chair of Online Degree in Biblical Studies
The Master's University

"Professor William Varner's work on Song of Solomon and Ecclesiastes is the best treatment of these books I have ever read—scholarly, orthodox, yet practical and uplifting. His treatment of the other 'poetic books' is also eye-opening. If I were to teach these books today, I would require Varner's book as the number one required reading. It opens up the reader's understanding to these under-appreciated works and gives them a clarity that applies to the Christian life in an uplifting manner."

**Gary G. Cohen, Th.D.**
Retired Seminary Professor and Army Chaplain

# The Preacher and the Song

# The Preacher and the Song

*William Varner*

Fontes

*The Preacher and the Song*

Copyright © 2023 by William Varner

ISBN-13: 978-1-948048-85-9 (paperback)

All rights reserved. No part of this publication may be reproduced, stored in a retrieval system, or transmitted in any form or by any means—electronic, mechanical, photocopy, recording, or any other—except for brief quotations in printed reviews, without the prior permission of the publisher.

Fontes Press
Dallas, TX
www.fontespress.com

*This book is dedicated to Robert Vandermey
who taught me how to be a pastor*

## Contents

Foreword, Dr. David W. Hegg ..... xi
Preface ..... xiii
1. Overview of Solomon's Life ..... 1
2. But What about Proverbs? ..... 15
3. The Challenge of the Song of Songs ..... 25
4. A Translation of the Song of Songs ..... 37
5. Ecclesiastes or the *Kohelet* ..... 61
6. Tracing the Goads and Nails ..... 75
7. The Preacher and the Song ..... 113

# Foreword

At the core of every biblical expositor's task is the challenge of taking an ancient message in an ancient language given to an ancient culture and bringing it to the audience of today. But the challenge doesn't stop there. Those who would preach the Word of God must not only cross the Grand Canyon of time but do so in ways that bring the ancient meaning of the text to bear on modern lives.

Because meaning is found in rightly discerning what the original author intended the original audience to understand from the words that he used, today's preacher faces an intimidating task. Given the demands of leadership, counseling, visitation, writing, Bible Studies, weddings, funerals, and a myriad of congregational expectations, those who preach every weekend rely on trusted scholars to do much of the historical heavy lifting. William Varner is one of those scholars, and the material in this small volume will not only introduce and unpack two enigmatic Old Testament books but leave the careful expositor ready to announce a preaching series through them.

His initial overview of Solomon's life is exceptionally useful. Solomon's perception, reflection, and understanding of life itself matured over time and is essential in sorting out the truths he expresses in both Song of Songs and Ecclesiastes.

This is especially true with Varner's explanation of the three-character scheme of Song of Songs. His view not only makes the best sense of the actual text but also does away with the pesky question of how King Solomon could ever be put forward as a model husband.

Varner's use of the Legacy Standard translation of both books, with his added nuances, is helpful both in his exactness and in his dividing the text into preaching sections.

Perhaps the greatest contribution made by Varner's careful yet accessible scholarship is his "goad and nail" paradigm as the guiding principle in understanding, interpreting, and applying Ecclesiastes. For years, we "every-weekend preachers" have struggled to deal with what seemed to be the overall negativity of this book. We've left it alone, thinking our people could not bear sermon after sermon on how meaningless life "under the sun" is in reality. But now Varner has come to our rescue. As he carefully unpacks the structure, Varner shows how the "goad" refers to a goading problem that is defined and illustrated by a series of proverbs before being followed by the "nail" which presents the wise and satisfying solution to the problem. This section alone is worth the price of the book.

As a biblical expositor I have no greater joy than preaching the Scriptures. If, like me, you believe that the Spirit of God uses the Word of God to do the work of God in the people of God, this volume will help you both to love and to preach Song of Songs and Ecclesiastes with confidence.

**Dr. David W. Hegg**
Senior Pastor
Grace Baptist Church
Santa Clarita, California

# Preface
## (to be read)

Later I will share with you my very first exposure as a young Christian to the Song of Songs, the actual title of the book (1:1). It was later in my second year at Bob Jones University that I first studied the book in an academic setting. I am very thankful that my professor and mentor was Dr. Fred Afman, who had just completed his dissertation titled "The Relationship of the Song of Solomon and Ecclesiastes to the Life of Solomon" (1966). Dr. Afman's approach to the Song was new to me, but it made sense of the book and it also fit into that king's rather checkered moral and spiritual life. Simply this approach is called "the three-character view," the characters being Solomon, the Shulamite, and the Shepherd. Although years later I was (wrongly) told by a Dallas Seminary professor that this was a higher critical view, I eventually discovered that a significant number of scholars with a high view of Scripture have endorsed this approach. We will examine this issue in a more in-depth way in this book.

At Faith and Biblical Theological Seminaries in the early 1970s, I explored further the perplexing Book of Ecclesiastes, or *Kohelet* as we will often call it. At BJU, Dr. Afman had also exposed me to a "positive" view of the book rather than negatively seeing it simply as the ruminations of "man under the sun." It was Professor Tom Taylor who convinced me in 1970 that a fair reading of 12:9–14 indicates that the whole book, including the negative sections, was what the author described as "words of truth" that were "given from one Shepherd." This assured me that the book itself justified its role in the Hebrew canon as inspired and authoritative. But I was still a bit perplexed by those negative passages, especially the ones that seemed to deny life after death, which Watchtower cultists liked to point out at my door! One day, and I forgot exactly when, I discovered an article by a professor at Calvin Seminary, Martin Wyngaarden. This author also pointed me to that same passage at the end of the book that likens the words of the wise to "goads" and "nails." Applying that to the rest of the book, it soon became clear that the many overlooked positive statements about God (forty of them) were part of the author's plan of presenting initially a negative "goad" followed by a positive "nail."

When I arrived in California in 1996, I soon became aware of an entire book by Richard De Haan that took a practical approach, working through Ecclesiastes in this way with the creative title, *The Art of Staying Off Dead-End Streets*. Since then, it has been my delight to teach and preach these books with the approach to them that I just outlined. My wife and I have verse references from Song of Songs 8 inscribed in our wedding rings and many a nervous but happy couple whom I married has heard my wedding sermon on 8:6–7! After many years of teaching these books, I think that I am now ready to share this approach with you readers.

As you can probably gather from its modest length, this book does not attempt to offer a detailed commentary on every verse in these works. To be honest with you, such commentaries, although based on the Hebrew texts, often turn out to produce more heat than light! One can almost choke on their detailed minutiae, while completely missing what we could call the "Big Idea." Very few commentators have tried to discover the internal features of the books that can help us to read them with comprehension and profit for our lives. I am convinced that the keys to the books, as well as to many other OT and NT books, are near their "back door." Rather than offering a detailed exegesis (and I have read the books in Hebrew!), my goal is to suggest a strategy for reading these books as a whole. I believe that the template that I offer for reading them is one that is drawn from the books themselves! If we break our heads over the details of a book but somehow miss the "Big Picture," we are simply wasting our time. Scholars have referred to my approach as "discourse analysis" and "grammar above the level of the sentence." This approach is simply an effort to view a text as a whole and not just as the sum total of its verses. I hope my method commends itself to you and that these books truly become part of your regular Scripture reading and study.

Many commentaries on Biblical texts often do not include the very Biblical texts they are seeking to explain. Because of this and because I want the readers to test out and verify what I am trying to say, I have included the full English texts of both books from the *Legacy Standard Bible*, along with my explanations of them. Ecclesiastes or *Kohelet* will be presented in the order of the "goads" and the following "nails" that I think emerge from the books.

No, the Song of Songs is not a "sex manual for believers" and Ecclesiastes is not just bemoaning how we ought *not* to live! While I do not buy into the allegorical approach, especially to the Song, I will also seek to draw spiritual lessons from the texts and discern if a valid typology can be detected in the characters portrayed. The practical lessons from Ecclesiastes will also be explored and applied. We finally will also try to see if the New Testament employs and applies these texts for our spiritual growth.

This book is written for the serious Bible reader, and not primarily for academics. Therefore, when I cite an author, I will simply mention the last name with the appropriate page numbers (e.g., Ginsburg, 4–6). The bibliographical details for that work will then be found at the end of that chapter. Finally, although I try to consistently use Song of Songs rather than Song of Solomon, for Ecclesiastes I admit to using both that traditional title as well as the transliterated Hebrew title, *Kohelet*. The text of *Legacy Standard Bible* is utilized except in a few rare places.

# 1

# Overview of Solomon's Life

## His Birth and Naming

Because one of the purposes of this book is an attempt to relate how both Ecclesiastes and the Song of Songs fit into what we know about Solomon's life, it is essential to be aware of what that life looked like, based on the OT texts which record his story. This chapter is a rather substantial summary of his life with comments on his "spirituality" as reflected in our sources. While the reader may desire to move ahead to the details of those important texts, Ecclesiastes and the Song of Songs, let me encourage you to review with me the details of his life that may have escaped you. It was in reading and reviewing Solomon's life that I actually changed my opinion about the order in which the three Solomonic books were written!

Solomon was the second son of David by Bathsheba although he was not the second son of David. Six sons had been born earlier from six different wives in Hebron, among them Amnon, Absalom, and Adonijah (2 Sam 3:25). Of nine sons born to David in Jerusalem, Solomon was probably the first (1 Chron 3:5–9), since he was the first son of Bathsheba to survive infancy (2 Sam 12:18).

The significance of his birth was overshadowed by David's sin and the judgment of continuing strife among his sons (2 Sam 12:9–12), but his birth was a sign to his parents of Yahweh's forgiveness of David and his restoration. The name "Solomon" (Heb *Shlomo*) means "peaceable" and indicates that David was a partaker in God's peace. It may also suggest that David's desire was that his son would enjoy what he had not experienced, namely a life of peace. It should not be overlooked that Yahweh's name for him was Jedidiah, according to a message from Nathan the prophet: "Now Yahweh loved him and ... he named him Jedidiah for the sake of Yahweh" (2 Sam 12:25). As David's name meant "beloved one," Solomon's "official" name meant "Beloved of Yahweh." This indicates that Yahweh loved Solomon and blessed David's eventual marriage to Bathsheba. The incident of the child's naming must have emerged like a burst of sunshine on what was a dark and gloomy day in the couple's experience.

### His Childhood

The training of the child is a matter of conjecture, and may have fallen to his mother, Bathsheba. This woman has often been unjustly maligned, for she probably had not much say in the matter when a powerful monarch had earlier sent and "took" her for himself (2 Sam 11:4). In any case, the prophet Nathan was probably the chief tutor of the young lad. While the record is actually silent on his actual training, there is no reason to suppose that spiritual influences were neglected. If we are correct in advocating the Solomonic authorship of much of Proverbs plus the astounding theology of his prayer in 1 Kings 8:22–53, his knowledge of the Torah, despite his eventual shortcomings, was obviously profound.

On the other hand, life in a polygamous Davidic palace must have negatively influenced the boy as he grew into adolescence and young manhood. The revolt of Absalom also occurred around his tenth year. Furthermore, the selfish actions of Amnon and Adonijah must have served as both warnings and instruction as to what should be expected of the future king. At the close of his first twenty years, Solomon was still Jedidiah, the Beloved of Yahweh, worthy of the throne and fit to be the builder of Yahweh's temple.

### His Early Years as King

With the added authority and responsibilities of the throne, Solomon did not forget his earlier training. His experiences with

God were evident from his anointing and from that previously mentioned prayer of dedication in 1 Kings 8.

Even in his final days, David at seventy had not been able to rest in peace. Solomon's anointing by Zadok emerged out of his half-brother Adonijah's anointing at En-Rogel and attempt to seize the kingdom (1 Kings 1). This son of Absalom completed the prophetic announcement by Nathan that David ironically would be punished fourfold, with four sons dying prematurely (2 Sam 12:6–12). David responded to the news of his son's plot by remembering his oath to Solomon to follow him on the throne (1 Kings 1:29–30). The offices of prophet and priest that were formerly combined in Samuel, now were fulfilled by two men: Zadok the priest and Nathan the prophet. As the rightful heir was anointed, Yahweh's spirit evidently came upon him as He had done with his father, David (1 Sam 16:13). The offices of prophet, priest, and king were to guard the Israelite theocracy, and the young king was now ready to take his anointed place and role. The city acclaimed him, his enemies were dispersed, and the rebel Adonijah was the first to experience the grace of the newly anointed king. By viewing Adonijah's flight to the horns of the altar as a confession and guilt and repentance, Solomon established himself as a monarch marked by clemency and wisdom.

Just as his predecessor David received a second anointing (1 Sam 16/2 Sam 5), Solomon's second anointing (1 Chron 29:22), unlike the earlier local and hasty event (1 Kings 1:38–39), marked the passing of David and the subsequent rallying of the people to him. The elderly David's charge was that he serve Yahweh with a perfect heart (1 Chron 28:9). The joy of the leaders and the people was climaxed as the young monarch was anointed publicly to be the new governor of the land. "Then Solomon sat on the throne of Yahweh as king instead of David his father; and he succeeded, and all Israel obeyed him" (1 Chron 29:23).

The admonition to Solomon contained instructions for the death of Joab the double-murderer and Shimei the blasphemer of Yahweh. The young king's punishment of these criminals, as harsh as it may sound to modern sensibilities, revealed his obedience to his "oath of office" and his defense of the throne of Yahweh.

Solomon did not have long to wait for an event to give proof of another's loyalty. The mercifully treated Adonijah's request for Abishag as his wife embodied his second attempt to usurp the throne. Marriage to the wife of the previous king would give him at least a claim to the throne. The new king quickly and wisely recognized this threat to his throne and tasked Benaiah to perform the ugly but needed execution (1 Kings 2:19–25). Joab's fleeing to the horns of the altar proved his implication in the plot and justice was finally also administered to this nephew of David (1 Kings 2:28–34). Shimei was granted a restricted stay in Jerusalem but after three years he broke his oath and was justly put to death (2:36–46). While to some modern readers this may sound like an ancient reign of terror, in actuality Solomon's actions proved him to be the man who could defend the laws of Yahweh as a worthy monarch on the throne of Yahweh. The merciful treatment of Barzillai (1 Kings 2:7) indicated a true balance and shows that he was not a revenge-seeking despot, but a just and honorable king. He exhibited a growth in his spirituality as God gave him grace and courage to enforce the laws. "Thus the kingdom was established in the hands of Solomon" (1 Kings 2:46).

## His Dream and Decision

Before describing one of the high points in Solomon's life, namely his request for wisdom at Gibeon, his marriage to a daughter of Pharaoh is mentioned as well as his sacrificing at the high places (1 Kings 3:1–4). It is not stated, however, that Yahweh was displeased with the marriage since she may have affirmed her faith in the one true God of Israel. The historian did not condemn this action, as he clearly would do in the case of the later wives, whose idolatry the king would tolerate and even encourage (1 Kings 11:1–2). His sacrificing at high places was not condemned either, because all people were doing the same thing since the central temple was not yet built. Furthermore, right after this statement appear verses which commend Solomon for his love of Yahweh, especially for his thousand sacrifices on the Gibeon altar (3:3–4). The paragraph ends with anything but a Divine condemnation: "In Gibeon,

## Overview of Solomon's Life

Yahweh appeared to Solomon in a dream at night; and God said, 'Ask what I should give to you.'" This certainly reflects a Divine approval of Solomon at this point.

Much could be said about the spiritual features of this prayer. He thanked Yahweh for His *hesed*, translated variously as "grace" or "mercy" or "covenant love" or "lovingkindness" (3:6). He thus acknowledged his own personal deficiencies (3:7). His older brothers had coveted the monarchy in arrogance, but the true heir trembled and admitted his unworthiness. He knew the great responsibility before him (3:8), so he acknowledged his need for an understanding heart and for the ability to discern between good and evil (3:9). With all of his abilities, he still prayed for wisdom, which if granted would be used for service and not for his own glory. In his last days, his father had stated that the one who rules people must be just, ruling in the fear of God (2 Sam 23:3). His son is now asking for the wisdom to do just that!

Yahweh's response to this prayer was marked by His pleasure and His provision. To borrow from a future prayer promise, He was pleased to do exceedingly more than Solomon asked because he sought first the kingdom of God and His righteousness. Eventually Solomon's wisdom would be as "the sand on the seashore" (4:29). The renown of his wisdom reached beyond his fellow Israelites (4:30), and the description was actually beyond all expectation in that "that there was none like you neither after you shall be anyone like you" (3:12), and thus he was granted wealth and fame.

That this wisdom was more than the accumulation of facts is evident by his judgment in the case of the two harlots (3:16–27), a grisly story whose final act has been captured by more than one artist. In a classic example of a "she said/she said" case, since there were no witnesses, the still youthful but wise king demonstrated that possessing wisdom means having insight into human nature. He knew that the real mother of the surviving child would never stand for her child being cut in two and shared by each woman! The effect of this wisdom beyond his age is carefully reflected in the summary statement following this wise and brilliant judgment. "Then all Israel heard of the judgment which the king had handed down, and they feared the king, for they saw that the wisdom of God was in him to do justice" (4:28). Such wisdom does not come from schools and classrooms; it is "the wisdom that comes from God."

True wisdom is reflected also in conduct, which is the main theme of Solomon's writings. Proverbs relates to the conduct of life in society; Ecclesiastes relates to conduct before God; and the Song of Songs relates to the conduct of love between a man and woman. It will be the task of the rest of this book to see where and how the books we call "the Preacher" and his "Song" fit into the life of Solomon as he grew older, but sadly not wiser!

## His Riches and Honor

Solomon had asked for grace, not for gold. After commending the young king for *not* asking for wealth, however, Yahweh promised him both riches and honor! This irony has always fascinated me. I suggest that it was a test. Will Solomon use his wealth wisely? The source of his wealth was from three things: taxes, commerce, and tribute. The management for the taxation program was under the care of an administration appointed for this purpose (1 Kings 4:1–6). The source of commerce was by land for the nearby neighbors Tyre, Egypt, and Arabia, while by sea it was possibly with countries as far away as today's Spain, India, and the coasts of Africa. The tribute came from surrounding countries with the expanding orbit of Israel. "And they brought every man his present, articles of silver and gold, garments, weapons, spices, horses, and mules, a set amount year by year" (1 Kings 10:25). The last clause indicates that this tribute was something fixed and regular.

One of the evidences for the Solomonic authorship of *Kohelet* (Ecclesiastes) is that the author refers to the greatness that he achieved in some of the following statements. "I have seen all the works which have been done under the sun, and behold, all is vanity and striving after wind" (Eccl 1:14). "I made my works great: I built houses for myself; I planted vineyards for myself; I made for myself gardens and parks, and I planted in them all kinds of fruit trees; I made for myself pools of water from which to water a forest of growing trees. I bought male and female slaves, and I had homeborn slaves. Also I possessed flocks and herds larger than all who preceded me in Jerusalem. Also, I collected for myself silver and gold and the treasure of kings and provinces. I provided for myself male and female singers and the pleasures of the sons of men—many concubines. Then I became great and increased more than all who preceded me in Jerusalem. My wisdom also stood by me" (2:4–9). If this is not Solomon, we do not know who could qualify to claim this.

The financial total of all of these enterprises was 666 talents of gold (1 Kings 10:14; 2 Chron 9:13). This was probably a yearly income and by today's equivalent standards would be over one billion dollars! It must be kept in mind that his great wealth was evidence of God's approval and would remind him of his responsibilities before God. A New Testament parallel would be Paul's admonishment to the rich that they were not guilty for being rich but were to see their wealth as a stewardship to share with others (1 Tim 6:17–19).

World-wide fame accompanied this wealth. Kings came to hear his wisdom (1 Kings 10:24) and at least one queen as well (Sheba, 1 Kings 10:1). No skeptical visitor to Jerusalem could honestly return home unimpressed with what they saw in Solomon's kingdom. The queen's testimony was that this was due to a divine blessing (10:9). This experience, still in the early part of his reign, is a testimony of Solomon's genuine spirituality at this period of his life—and should have been a warning to him as well! Everything he had—life, throne, wealth, fame, wisdom—he had received from Yahweh. This needs to be remembered later in this volume when we see his statements about the futility of it all in *Kohelet*! But that is yet to come!

Length of life, however, was dependent on Solomon's obedience. "Now if you walk in My ways, keeping My statutes and commandments, as your father David walked, then I will prolong your days" (1 Kings 3:14). Although he is described as "old" in 11:4, this probably means "older" because he never attained the age of his father, and probably died around the age of sixty. His royal reign was as long as his father's, but not the years of his actual life. Sin shortened his days. But again we are getting ahead of ourselves!

The young king did not forget to show his gratitude for the promises and privileges that were his. In Jerusalem, the location of the ark, he offered burnt offerings and peace offerings. He praised God for the gifts he had received, for those he would receive, and rejoiced in the grace of God. To this was granted the blessing of peace with those "enemies" around him. This outward peace led to the idyllic description of inner peace within as well: "... and he had peace on all sides around about him. So Judah and Israel lived in security, every man under his vine and his fig tree, from Dan even to Beersheba, all the days of Solomon" (4:24b–25). These expressions denote the security and the satisfaction of enjoying the fruits of one's labors. The description of a person under his vine and fig tree came later to denote the tranquility and true shalom that would not reach this extent again until the coming of the Messiah and His kingdom (Micah 4:4; Zech 3:10; see also the allusion to this in John 1:48, 50).

The peace of this Solomonic/Messianic reign is also celebrated in one of the two canonical psalms attributed to him (72, see also 127). This beautiful composition is classified as a Royal Messianic Psalm, dealing with the future reign of the Messiah. While Yahweh had made a covenant with David about his throne and His king, and although Solomon did have a reign of peace that was typical of Messiah's kingdom, he did not fulfill all of the covenant blessings. Thus, there will be a literal fulfillment by the ultimate Son of David which will encompass the entire world!

## His Building and Dedication of the Temple

In the inspired record of Solomon's reign, pride of place is given to his construction of the temple, taking up no fewer than four chapters (1 Kings 5–8). Because of space, we can only summarize the rest of the account of the king, including his triumphs and his tragedies. The location for the temple had already been secured through the purchase by David of Araunah's threshing floor on Mt. Moriah (2 Sam 24). David had prepared the site, gathered the building materials, including the precious metals and stones, and had secured an agreement from Hiram, king of Tyre, that the Phoenician king would supply the cedar timber as well as the workers needed to erect the temple.

The basic pattern of the temple, though no specifications are provided, appears to be identical to that of the Mosaic tabernacle. This much larger structure, however, was seven years in its construction under the supervision of Huram-Abi. The description of its gold and other resplendent features is so breathtaking that some have doubted that anyone, much less a monarch like Solomon, could have had access to this much wealth. But there is no reason to doubt the abundant blessings supplied by Yahweh, Whom he was faithfully serving at this time. Like the earlier tabernacle, the plan for the buildings included three sections: a portico or outer court (*ulam*), a sanctuary or holy place (*kodesh*), and a holy of holies (*dvir*). The patient reader can read the details of all this in the descriptions of the temple in 1 Kings 5:16–7:38 and 2 Chron 4. The construction's climax was the bringing of the ark into the temple's Holy of Holies (8:1–11). It had previously been located in the tent of meeting in the lower part of the city since it had been brought up from Kirjath-Jearim by David (2 Sam 6).

Rather than spend the reader's time on the details of this structure, some attention must be given to his amazing prayer of dedication because it motivates our purpose in describing his spirituality at this point in his early career. Solomon's astounding dedicatory prayer is recorded in 1 Kings 8:22–53 and in 2 Chron 6. This prayer illustrates the heights from which he was later to fall! The Chronicler includes some preparatory details to be noted. He stood before the altar (2 Chron 6:12), he knelt down, and he spread his hands toward heaven (6:13). He did these things publicly, not to be seen by others, but to represent the people since he was in the temple. The prayer expresses his attitude toward Yahweh, toward himself, toward the temple, and toward the people. Solomon declares that the God of Israel is beyond comparison, and he thanks Him for all He has done for Solomon's people. He echoes themes found in the Torah, thus proving that the King was familiar with the words of the Law as commanded in Deut 17:18: "Now it will be when he sits on the throne of his kingdom, that he shall write for himself a copy of this law on a scroll in the presence of the Levitical priests." I personally read this with a bit of pain because I wonder if the neglect of having that scroll near him daily was the cause of his later defection! There are many echoes of Deuteronomy throughout the prayer (see, for example, Deut 6:13; 28:22, 23, 25), but these can be augmented by other references in Exodus, Leviticus, and even Numbers. If no other proofs were available, his prayer would be sufficient to portray Solomon as a deeply spiritual man at this stage in his life and career.

Solomon concludes by requesting that Yahweh would enter His temple, and his last words to the people were marked by a dramatic event that convinced the people and Solomon that the One to whom he prayed was pleased. When the tabernacle had been completed centuries before, Yahweh entered it by consuming the sacrifice on the altar by fire. Similarly, at the conclusion of Solmon's prayer, according to 2 Chron 7:1, "the glory of Yahweh filled the house," thus indicating that He was pleased with the king, the people, and the temple. Both king and people then expressed their joy by offering sacrifices in abundance. 2 Chron 7:10 concludes eloquently by saying that Solomon "sent the people to their tents, with gladness and goodness of heart because of the goodness that Yahweh had shown to David and to Solomon and to Israel His people."

### His Building Projects

When Solomon had finished constructing the temple, he turned to building his own magnificent palace. While the temple took seven years to build, Solomon's own palace took thirteen (1 Kings 6:38; 7:1), meaning that both projects consumed twenty years (1 Kings 9:10). Thus, the temple was completed by around 959 BC and the palace in 946 BC. Solomon constructed his palace with timber from the forests of Lebanon, and it was larger than the temple. It had wings such as the hall of justice as well as Solomon's private quarters. In addition, the daughter of Pharoah (Siamun?), who was married to Solomon, was given her own palace, for she had been residing in temporary facilities in the "City of David."

In other projects, the king built a wall around the original town of Jebus on the southern Ophel Ridge and enclosed the area of the temple and the public buildings on the north for the first time. The total area enclosed was only about one thousand yards from north to south and two hundred yards from east to west. This was not large by modern norms, but it was a significant city and sanctuary by ancient standards. Solomon also worked on filling the terraces of this lower ridge—Ophel being a word meaning "filling"—on the slopes built on the sides of the hill. This provided more space for other buildings and for defensive structures such as city walls.

Construction was not limited to Jerusalem, for Solomon fortified chariot cities such as Hazor, Megiddo, and Gezer (1 Kings 9:15). Each city was strategically located on a trade route later called the "Via Maris" (Way of the Sea) and each also served as a military facility. Excavations of all three sites have yielded evidence of Solomon's presence, including amazing water tunnels and fortifications illustrating his military prowess. At Megiddo, for example, have been found the installations at least built over stables from the time of Solomon. The stables consisted of rows of long narrow rooms separated by a solid wall, with each group of three rooms divided only by a monolithic pillar that had holes, presumably for tethering the horses, plus stone containers identified as mangers between the pillars. These accommodations could provide for three squadrons of chariot horses, each squadron consisting of fifty chariot-teams of three horses each, making a total of 450 horses.

Solomon even refortified towns outside the earlier boundaries of Israel as far away as the Orontes River to the north and others 140 miles northeast of Damascus. These served as a defensive chain of locations "in Lebanon and throughout all the territory he ruled" (1 Kings 9:19). Without a doubt he was a master builder, rivalled only by a much later king named Herod! Solomon's construction of the Jerusalem temple, however, consolidated the relationship between Israel's political and religious arms by the centrality of the sanctuary. Yahweh was the real monarch, and the king was Yahweh's vice-regent. The ornateness of this temple, as well as the amazing decoration and ornamentation of the other royal buildings, portrayed the vast riches of the kingdom and delivered that message to the people.

Divine grace had been evidenced in the life of Solomon from his birth through the first twenty years of his reign as king. He had carried honorably the name Jedidiah, Beloved of the Lord. His early training by Nathan the prophet had imparted discernment and discipline in him. He had experienced the guidance of the Holy Spirit (*Ruach haKodesh*). His walk and worship marked him as a spiritual man endowed with spiritual gifts. Yahweh honored the building of the Temple by placing His name there through the flame of the *Shekinah* Glory. Israel had a king endowed with the gifts of wisdom, wealth, and fame, along with the divine approval and presence. Although the following could not serve as a final epitaph on his tomb, at this point it could justly be written about him: "So King Solomon became greater than all the kings of the earth in riches and in wisdom. And all the earth was seeking the presence of Solomon, to hear his wisdom which God had put in his heart" (1 Kings 10:23–24).

## The Decline of Solomon

Solomon's last years were not at all like his earliest days. In actuality his empire began to fall apart before his very eyes. The ultimate reason was spiritual: "Now Yahweh was angry with Solomon because his heart was turned away from Yahweh, the God of Israel, who had appeared to him twice, and had commanded him concerning this thing, that he should not walk after other gods; but he did not keep what Yahweh had commanded" (1 Kings 11:9–10). At the root of his problems were his multiple marriage alliances with other nations so sadly portrayed in the passage immediately preceding (11:1–8). While the marriages were part of political treaties with pagan rulers, these loveless but still forbidden alliances required him to provide for their foreign pantheons in the heart of the land in order to pacify his wives. The chapter mentions that Solomon built sanctuaries for Molech and Chemosh on the mountain east of Jerusalem (11:7–8). This hill directly east of the ancient City of David is referred to today as the "Mount of Shame" because of these detestable associations. When we eventually examine the details in the Song of Songs, we will see that "the daughters of Jerusalem" portrayed at various intervals (2:7; 3:5; 5:8, 16; 8:4) are the voices of this Oriental harem.

As a result of this departure from Yahweh, He "raised up an adversary to Solomon…" (1 Kings 11:14). The first such was Hadad the Edomite. It was perhaps the height of irony that Pharaoh gave his daughter to Solomon as a wife, who was the sister-in-law to Solomon's most resolute enemy, Hadad. Hadad returned to Edom after the news of David and Joab's death (1 Kings 11:21). When the Edomites are mentioned again, some seventy-five years later, they are loosely under the control of Jehoshaphat, king of Judah (1 Kings 22:47). A second adversary was Rezin of Damascus, who had been a vassal of Hadadezer when David defeated the king of Zobah; but now Rezin had established his own power base in Damascus. While Damascus was still theoretically under Israel's rule, Rezin became a constant thorn in Solomon's side. The crumbling of these alliances stands in stark contrast with his international power described in such effusive language earlier in 1 Kings.

The bright day of Solomon's glory was darkening into clouds and gloom. His decline and fall from his high estate are indeed a sad record and can be a shock to beginning readers of this up-till-now heroic saga. As was noted earlier, chief among the causes of his decline were his polygamy and his great wealth. As he grew older he spent more of his time among his favorites. The increasingly idle king lived among these idle women with all their mischievous attendants, filling the palaces and pleasure-houses which he had built (1 Kings 11:3). He doubtless learned first to tolerate and then to imitate their heathen ways. He did not cease to believe in the God of Israel with his mind, and he probably continued to offer the prescribed sacrifices in the temple at the great festivals, but his heart was not right with God. His worship undoubtedly became formal; his soul, emptied by the cooling of true religious fervor, sought to be filled with any excitement which offered itself. Now for the first time a worship was publicly set up amongst the people of Yahweh, one which was not simply irregular or forbidden, like that of Gideon (Judg 8:27) or the Danites (Judg. 18:30–31), but one that was downright idolatrous (1 Kings 11:7; 2 Kings 23:13).

For forty years Solomon ruled his people, but the seeds of defection from the union had been well established in his own day. Though he would die before the fruit of some of his own disastrous policies would come to fruition, the division of the kingdom was now beyond repair or remediation. This judgment was announced in 11:11: "So Yahweh said to Solomon, 'Because this has happened with you: you have not kept My covenant and My statutes, which I have commanded you, *so* I will surely tear the kingdom from you, and will give it to your servant. Nevertheless, I will not do it in your days for the sake of your father David, *but* I will tear it out of the hand of your son.'"

Solomon's true heir was Rehoboam, born from Naamah the Ammonitess, the fruit of another of his "political marriages" (14:21). The rival referred to in the prophetic condemnation in 11:11 was Jeroboam the son of Nebat, a former trusted member of Solomon's cabinet. He had been promoted to the rank of overseer of labor in the district of Ephraim (11:27–28) after Solomon had noticed his industry and abilities while building the Millo at Jerusalem. But when the prophet Ahijah met Jeroboam one day and informed him that he would be given the ten northern tribes to rule over as a result of Solomon's apostate ways, then Jeroboam found it necessary to flee to Egypt to save his life when word about this prophecy leaked out. Pharaoh Shishak (945–924 BC) gave him sanctuary (11:40), and there Jeroboam waited until the death of Solomon to become the first king of the Northern Kingdom of Israel.

We have only briefly surveyed this last period of Solomon's life, because it sadly is the best-known segment of his life among most Bible readers. It is during this period of perhaps twenty-five years that we will attempt to locate the writings for which he is known, the Song of Songs and Ecclesiastes. His contributions to the Book of Proverbs, while not the main concern of this volume, must be considered and located as well.

2

# But What about Proverbs?

I want to be very clear that the book before you is primarily about how Ecclesiastes and the Song of Songs fit into the life of King Solomon. I also plan to offer an explanation of the contents of those two books through an approach to each that may be new to the reader. But there is another book in the Old Testament canon that is also attributed to that Israelite king, and that is the Book of Proverbs. Well, not all of the book is credited to him, but the expression "the proverbs of Solomon" appears at 1:1; 10:1; and 25:1. We also read that 22:17–24:22 is titled "The Sayings of the Wise" as well as 24:23–34. Chapter 30 is credited to an unknown named "Agur" and at least part of 31 is credited to "King Lemuel," although that person is unknown and may even be a pseudonym for Solomon.

I see no reason to doubt the book's claim that the essential author was Solomon, son of David. Critics will always want to have their say, but I promise you that I will not spend time trying to defend the book's internal claim of authorship. The historical record powerfully states the following.

> And God gave Solomon wisdom and very great discernment and breadth of understanding in his heart, like the sand that is on the seashore. And Solomon's wisdom surpassed the wisdom of all the sons of the east and all the wisdom of Egypt. ... **He also spoke 3,000 proverbs, and his songs were 1,005.** And he spoke of trees, from the cedar that is in Lebanon even to the hyssop that grows on the wall; he spoke also of animals

and birds and creeping things and fish. And men came from all peoples to hear the wisdom of Solomon, from all the kings of the earth who had heard of his wisdom (1 Kings 4:29–34).

With that amazing accolade, who am I or anyone else to claim that we know more than the ancient authors about the literary output of this man? While my book is primarily about the final two works of his literary triad, *Kohelet* (the Hebrew for Ecclesiastes) and Song of Songs, I offer now a small chapter on how Proverbs fits into the life that we surveyed in the last chapter. This effort will also give me an opportunity to briefly consider each of the five works which are commonly called the "Poetic Books" (adding Job and Psalms) and how they perform a literary role among the Poetic Books that is often overlooked.

## The Key Near the Back Door

I once heard a saying that the key to a Biblical book is often found hanging near its back door. While that may not be a good practice for your house, it often is the case that the end of a canonical book will provide not only a key but a brief summary of its contents. While Job and Psalms were not written by Solomon (except for Psalms 72 and 127), they are part of the Poetic Books that in our English Bibles are in the order: Job, Psalms, Proverbs, Ecclesiastes, Song of Songs. A brief look at how this plays out in the first two will be followed by how it works in the final three.

## Job and Psalms

The **Book of Job** is in the shape of a literary *inclusio*: chapters 1–2 and the end of chapter 42 are written in prose with thirty-nine chapters in between in poetry. The conclusion indicates that the so-called "friends" of Job had not spoken what was right about Job's trials (42:7). This helps us to peruse the earlier discourses by Eliphaz, Bildad, and Zophar with a justifiably critical eye and be careful about heedlessly quoting a text from their diatribes as if it conveys the truth! Job had made some amazing theological statements about the Lord (e.g., 19:25–27), but even he does not speak perfectly in every passage. The conclusion also helps us to be a bit patient with Job who may have wanted at times to challenge the Deity to a debate. We should also remember that he was not aware of the events described for the reader in chapters 1 and 2. This key at the back door also indicates how the roles of Job and his friends are reversed. None of them previously had realized that they, not Job, could be the objects of Divine wrath and in need of His grace (42:7). In a delightful irony, they now discover that unless they secure the intercession of Job, they will not escape God's displeasure, which displeasure they had earlier preached to Job!

These and other statements in the epilogue not only tie the story back to the early chapters but also set the entire book in the period of the Patriarchs in Genesis. An often overlooked monetary detail is obscured by the rendering in most versions by "piece of money" for a Hebrew word in 42:11: "Then all his brothers and all his sisters and all who had known him before came to him, and they ate bread with him in his house; and they consoled him and comforted him for all the calamity that Yahweh had brought on him. And each one gave him one *qesitah*, and each a ring of gold." The Legacy Standard Bible's unfamiliar rendering to English readers, *qesitah*, rather than the bland "piece of money" in most versions, should alert to the reader to the patriarchal currency mentioned only in Gen 33:19 and Josh 24:32, the last being a reference back to the patriarchal events.

Job's prayer to turn away the divine displeasure from the wicked also recalls a patriarchal intercession for the wicked in Sodom (Gen 18). Finally, there is the simple description of Job's dignified ending. "And after this, Job lived 140 years and saw his sons and his grandsons, four generations. Then Job died, an old man and full of days" (42:17–18). Readers should not rush by that closing without recalling the peaceful passings of the Genesis patriarchs as a sort of Israelite ideal (Gen 25:8; 35:19; 49:33; 50:26). This could even be true for a "Gentile" like Job who did not trace his lineage from Abraham through Isaac to Jacob and Joseph—notice, this is also four generations!

The significant ending to Job with its keys to its interpretation continues in its successor, the **Book of Psalms**. Psalm 150, which closes the book, is brief but filled with repetitions of one word, "praise." Count the times that this word appears in the following quotation of the psalm.

Praise Yah!
Praise God in His sanctuary;
Praise Him in His mighty expanse.
Praise Him for His mighty deeds;
Praise Him according to the abundance of His greatness.
Praise Him with trumpet blast;
Praise Him with harp and lyre.
Praise Him with tambourine and dancing;
Praise Him with stringed instruments and pipe.
Praise Him with resounding cymbals;
Praise Him with clashing cymbals.
Let everything that has breath praise Yah.
Praise Yah!

There are thirteen occurrences of the verb "to praise" in only six verses! The place where His praise is preeminent (His sanctuary); the world where He is be praised (His mighty expanse); the means by which He is praised (the musical instruments), and finally His people who are to praise (everything that breathes) are all included in this back door key that again echoes the dozens of times in the Psalter that readers should praise Yahweh. The preceding references to such praises in the book are too many to list! While the first four books of Psalms each end in a verse or two of doxology, the fifth rounds off the whole Psalter with an entire psalm of praise.

The praise of God in this final paean of praise opens with a call to praise Him in the mighty expanse of His (heavenly) sanctuary (150:1) and brings to a resounding conclusion some themes of the immediately preceding psalms. He reigns across all generations (146:10). He builds up Jerusalem (147:2). His heavenly host praise Yahweh from the heavens and heights (148:1–2). His splendor is above earth and heaven (148:13). Earthly Zion rejoices in the One who rules as King (149:2). These all prepare the reader and singer to affirm that the Divine sanctuary is His mighty expanse (150:1). In this way the "back door psalm" is the final "stanza" in a doxology that consists of Psalms 146–150!

Readers of this inspired and inspiring collection know that there are different types or genres of psalms—penitential, messianic, worship, thanksgiving, lament, didactic, *hallel*, ascent. But if there is one word that could bind them all together it is the word "praise," and that is the key that is so prominent on the back door of Psalm 150. Perhaps that is why the one-word title of this variegated collection chosen by the rabbis to describe it is *Tehillim*, which simply means "Praises." That is the one key at the end that unlocks the door to the entire collection.

One almost feels apologetic for these brief treatments of Job and Psalms, but we remind the reader that the main concern of this volume is with the writings traditionally associated with Solomon, to which we now turn. The main subject of this current chapter is Proverbs and again we turn to the back door of that book for some insight into its overall message.

## Proverbs

The very last section of Proverbs has to do with that famous description of the *eshet hay'il*, the woman whose accompanying adjective has been translated variously as "virtuous" (KJV, NKJV) and "excellent" (LSB, NASB) and "noble" (NIV) and "courageous" (meaning of LXX) and "capable" (NRS, CSB). It has always been fascinating to this professor that the adjective *hay'il* is the same word used to described the male heroes in Judges as "mighty men of *valor*" (3:29; 6:12; 11:1; 18:2). This usage would tend toward the meaning of "brave" which was conveyed by the ancient Greek equivalent in the Septuagint ("courageous"). One could even render it as "strong" and that certainly could be true of the Proverbs 31 woman, who had to be strong to accomplish all that she does.

Many a Mother's Day sermon or other exhortation to women has portrayed the Proverbs 31 woman as the model for women in all ages. A survey of honest women, however, might reveal that many a Christian woman can get rather discouraged about ever living up to what I could call "Superwoman" as she is portrayed as the ultimate wife, mother, teacher, cook, investor, and all-around, let me say it again, "Superwoman." But where does that leave the married woman who has been unable to have children or the single woman or the Christian woman not blessed with a believing husband? Let me suggest another approach to the "back door" of Proverbs that is consistent with the way that one her best traits, wisdom (31:26), is portrayed in the book. With this brief background, I offer the following suggestion: that the woman in Proverbs 31 is intended by Solomon to portray the personification of wisdom, not to describe any actual woman on the face of God's earth. I know that this will be a challenge to many readers, so hear my case before you set this book aside.

The argument that the woman in Proverbs 31 is a personification of wisdom is not based on the occasional frustration of women falling short of her example. It is based on the amazing connections that her character and behavior traits share with the way wisdom is personified earlier in Proverbs. Ascribing personal traits to objects or to types of people is not uncommon in the Old Testament. Mountains and trees sing and clap hands (Isa 55:12), and in Proverbs the tongue hates (26:28). It is not surprising that wisdom is personified as a woman in this book, especially since the Hebrew noun *hokmah* is feminine. Wisdom, like a woman, can be attractive, and since a man can be attracted to a woman's beauty, so we all should be attracted to wisdom. Such a figure also heightens the way that folly and wisdom are contrasted, especially in chapters 8 and 9. Just as an immoral woman can lead men into ultimate "death" (9:13–18), so folly can lead people to follow foolish behavior that results in death.

Wisdom is also clearly personified in Proverbs as a prophetess (1:20–23); she is a sister (7:4); she is as one born (8:22–31); and, as mentioned above, she is a hostess (9:1–6). Proverbs 8 is a classic presentation of the personification of wisdom: she is priceless (vv. 10–11); she provides discretion (vv. 12–14); offers justice for rulers (vv. 15–16), plus insures wealth and honor (vv. 17–21). Like a woman, Wisdom is to be loved (vv. 17–21), which again suggests how appropriate it is for personifying her as a woman. Much more could be said about "her" role in 8:22–31.

As we arrive finally at Proverbs 31, consider these many links to previous statements about wisdom in the book. The "wife" is more precious than rubies (31:10) as also is wisdom (3:15; 8:11; cf. also 16:16). The *eshet hay'il* laughs in confidence at any future threat (31:25), and wisdom also laughs confidently at both real and possible disasters (1:26). Her lamp does not go out at night (31:18), while the light of the righteous is portrayed as always shining (13:9). In chapter 31 she is a wife of virtue and hard work, while in 9:1–6 Lady Wisdom prepares a banquet for young men. In 31:26 she provides instruction, and there are many earlier passages throughout Proverbs 1–9 where wisdom gives instruction. She also cares for the needy and teaches them, an element that parallels many passages about wisdom in the opening chapters, such as similar expressions found in 3:13–18 and 9:1–6. Her emphasis on the "fear of Yahweh" (31:30), recalls one of wisdom's very first fruits (1:7).

This last feature, which finds parallels in both the opening and ending sections, reminds us of the very first subject that is mentioned in 1:2: "wisdom." Not surprisingly, the last mention of this subject in the book is also present in this woman. "She opens her mouth in wisdom, and the instruction of lovingkindness is on her tongue" (31:26). This raises the distinct probability that the wisdom that is both portrayed and personified functions as a literary *inclusio* for the entire Book of Proverbs. Therefore, wisdom serves to bookend the entire treatise which expounds that subject in dozens of concrete ways throughout its pages. I would warn any interpreter about too quickly imposing a man-made structure on God's word, but the evidence listed above (which could even be expanded) ought to convince the careful reader that wisdom is not imposed as the *inclusio*, but rather leaps out at the careful reader. Here is a key that is near *both* the front and the back doors of this book!

Before we try to locate Proverbs within Solomon's life and career, we should look at one other reference to Lady Wisdom. In the Hebrew Bible, the books that we call the Old Testament are arranged in a different canonical order. The Book of Ruth immediately follows the book of Proverbs. Ruth embodies the kind of woman that King Lemuel tells his son to seek at the end of Proverbs. In fact, upon seeing her faithfulness to her mother-in-law Naomi and to Yahweh, Boaz calls Ruth an *eshet chayil* (3:11), even though Proverbs was written centuries after the Book of Ruth. What is interesting is that the lady Ruth does *not* exhibit some of the details mentioned in Proverbs 31. At the time in which such an honor is bestowed upon her, Ruth is neither a wife nor a mother—the epitome of femininity enshrined in much church culture today. Moreover, she is not a wealthy landowner with a household full of servants to oversee (like the Proverbs 31 woman). She is a widow and a foreigner on the margins of society. The text highlights Ruth's bravery in accompanying Naomi on a perilous journey to a foreign land without the protection of a man. It also shows how she embodied loyal love by selflessly caring for her bereaved mother-in-law. Single, married, childless, widowed, divorced—none are beyond the merit of such a title. Thanks to Angie Velasquez Thornton, for some of these stimulating thoughts about Ruth.

Therefore, we see in Proverbs 31 that Lady Wisdom gets the last word—the book of Proverbs retains its use of a woman to personify wisdom. Proverbs 31 is therefore one final, female, poetic description of Lady Wisdom, which both men and women are to seek equally.

But the truly last word on wisdom is not in Ruth or in Proverbs, but in the inspired words of a much later Jewish man named Jacob. No, he was not that patriarch in Genesis, but the brother of Jesus. Yes, that was his name, and it is preserved that way in Hebrew, Greek, and Latin. Somehow in medieval English it was changed to "James." His ultimate description follows. "But the wisdom from above is first pure, then peaceable, considerate, submissive, full of mercy and good fruits, without doubting, without hypocrisy" (James 3:17). If we did not know better, we might conclude after reading that richly expressed sentence that we were reading Proverbs!

We will soon move to the remaining chapters of the book before you, where we will examine the meaning of both the Song of

Songs and Ecclesiastes and how those books fit into Solomon's life. But first we should briefly ask how this pre-eminent wisdom book that we call Proverbs also fits into his life. I call attention again to the previous chapter where we extensively surveyed that life as it is unfolded in Kings and Chronicles. One answer to our question is the traditional response of the Jewish rabbis about where this triad of Solomonic books should be located in his life:

> Solomon wrote the Song with its stress on love, in his youth; Proverbs, with its emphasis on practical problems, in mid-life; and Ecclesiastes, with its characteristic pessimism, in old age. (*Shir Hashirim Rabbah*)

So, according to the rabbis, the chronological order of the Big Three Solomonic books was (1) Song of Songs, followed by (2) Proverbs, and then by (3) Ecclesiastes. I taught this suggested order for years in my Old Testament Survey II course, but the researching and the writing of this book have led me to conclude that this order just does not make sense in light of what we can read so clearly in the Book of Kings. In those books we saw how the initial fifteen years of the king's reign (ages 20 to 35) were marked by clear examples of his spirituality exemplified in both his words and his actions (1 Kings 3–8). How is it that Solomon's sixty wives and eighty concubines that are mentioned in Song 6:8 fit together with the godly example that he shows to us in those chapters in Kings? It appears to me that the wise teaching in the Proverbs better portrays the life context of his earlier years as mentioned above. My suggestion is that the Song was written after sliding into that carnal period of mid-life (1 Kings 9–11), probably around ages 35 to 50, that the Song clearly and sadly describes. Then the final period, probably around the ages 50 to 60, provides the context for what we will see reflected in Ecclesiastes, when his harem grew from this "smaller" number mentioned in Song 6:8 to the seven hundred wives and three hundred concubines mentioned in 1 Kings 11:3! It is in that last period that he reviews with regret his many foolish forays down dead-end streets! Despite the rabbinic quote above, the order in which we are studying these books—Proverbs, Song of Songs, Ecclesiastes—is the order in which they appear in most Hebrew Bibles (with "Ruth" of course inserted after Proverbs because she is called *eshet chayil* in 3:11).

We will be giving much more attention in the coming chapters to those last two eras in the king's life and the books that inhabited them. For now, however, let us celebrate the joys and blessings of the early part of his reign, when he not only taught the "Precepts of Proverbs" but evidently lived them out in both his public and in his private life.

# 3

# The Challenge of the Song of Songs

## A Personal Experience

My first experience with the Old Testament book that is most often called The Song of Solomon is almost embarrassing to relate. I was at a Christian summer camp in Tennessee the summer after my senior year in high school. I had been a believer for only about a year and knew little about the Bible and what I did know was mostly in the New Testament. One afternoon I walked into the large open room of the camp lodge and immediately saw and heard a group of my fellow male teens sitting in the corner with their Bibles open. I wanted to join this apparent "Bible study" but as I approached the small group, I thought it was strange that they were laughing among themselves as they were pointing to the pages of their Bibles. Then I heard one of them exclaim, "Can you believe that it says that?" As I joined them, I soon learned that they were looking at (studying is not quite the best verb) that little OT book that is the subject of this chapter. I honestly do not remember much that I learned from that experience except surprise that there was a Bible book that spoke explicitly about a man admiring a woman's breasts!

I am not the first Bible student to ask some of the following questions. What do we make of a book of Holy Scripture that opens with a description of kissing (1:2) and then mentions a private bedroom chamber (1:4)? Well, I learned that these references were mild as I continued to read about lying between a woman's breasts (1:13); intimate embracing (2:6); seeking one's love in bed

(3:1); admiring a woman's body (4:5); disrobing (5:3); describing private parts (7:2–7); and close embracing (8:3). I realize that compared to some of the extreme pornography available today, these passages are mild. But what is their role in a book that is supposed to be known for its spiritual message? Did God write a sex manual for us, as well as a guide to eternal salvation?

I soon learned that both Jews and Christians have struggled to comprehend this little poetic gem of eight chapters. In that basic work of religious Judaism called the Mishnah the revered Rabbi Akiba solemnly stated, "In the entire world there is nothing to equal the day on which the Song of Songs was given to Israel. All the Writings (*Ketuvim*) are holy, but the Song of Songs is the holy of holies" (*Yadaim* 3:5). During my early years as a Christian, I was weaned on the *Old Scofield Reference Bible*. I could also say that I cut my teeth and fed my young Christian soul on that KJV Bible and have it in a pride of place on my bookshelf fifty-seven years later. As I perused those notes for this book, I read the following comforting words from Scofield: "Nowhere in Scripture does the unspiritual mind tread upon ground so mysterious and incomprehensible, while the saintliest men and women of all ages have found in it a source of pure and exquisite delight."

So I decided to move slowly on the study of this strange but fascinating little book, not realizing that many years later I would hear about a popular pastor who travelled around delivering seminars on this book which he *did* approach as a sex manual, at least for married couples! But I could not move slowly on this book because by my nineteenth year I studied it as part of an Old Testament Survey course taught by Dr. Fred Afman at Bob Jones University. It is his unpublished dissertation on Song of Songs and Ecclesiastes that has helped to shape my "different" approach to these two books and that has led to the writing of this book. Little did I know during that course that someday my wife would have inscribed inside our wedding rings the following: "8-28-71 Song 8:6–7." But more about that later!

## Title and Author

Every treatment of a book in a Bible survey course begins with questions about the correct title and its author. We do not have to read far to learn the following. Although the book is most often called the Song of Solomon, in 1:1 we read: "The Song of Songs, which is Solomon's." In other words the book's title is the self-referenced expression "Song of Songs." This is the way that Hebrew expresses what we call in English the "superlative" form of an adjective. In other words, if the simple form is "pretty," the comparative form is "prettier," and the superlative form is "prettiest." Although making room for irregular adjectives like good, better, best, we usually add est to the adjective to form the superlative. Hebrew does the same by first mentioning the noun and then the plural form of that noun. Think of the following: "slave of slaves" as lowest slave (Gen 9:25); "holy of holies" as most holy place (Exod 26:33); "vanity of vanities" as worst vanity (Eccl 1:2); "Lord of lords" as greatest Lord (Deut 10:17). This Song of Songs is Solomon's "Best Song." Since 1 Kings 4:32 states that Solomon spoke 3,000 proverbs and 1,005 songs, this song was his best, the "song of songs." (The Hebrew is *Shir Hashirim*.)

Identifying the author is fairly easy, since his name follows in the first verse: "which is Solomon's." The Hebrew *leShlomoh* is most naturally translated that way, thus attributing King Solomon as the author. The expression is used the same way in crediting Solomon as the author of Psalms 72 and 127 in the "titles" of those psalms. Scholars will remind us that the expression could also mean "for Solomon" or "about Solomon," and that question will become a factor in our later discussion of the number of named characters that we find in the book.

Apart from 1:1 what can we learn about the author in the book itself? The author displays an amazing knowledge of "fauna" and "flora." About 15 species of animals and 21 varieties of plants are mentioned. In this regard notice what is mentioned about Solomon right after the reference in Kings to his many proverbs and songs. "And he spoke of trees, from the cedar that is in Lebanon even to the hyssop that grows on the wall; he spoke also of animals and birds and creeping things and fish" (1 Kings 4:33). Furthermore, the author displays great familiarity with the geography of the entire land of ancient Israel. From Jerusalem to Lebanon over a dozen sites are named, some of which are familiar and some which are not, possibly because they went by more than one name (Kedar, Sharon, Gilead, Amamo, Senir, Hermon, Tirzah, Heshbon, Carmel, Baal-Hamon). Familiarity with such separated locations in the north and the south also reflects a time for its writing before the division of the kingdom in 930 BC.

In addition to Solomon's name which appears six more times (1:5; 3:7, 9, 11; 8:11–12), on three occasions a figure is identified as a "king" (1:4, 12; 7:5). The cumulative force of this evidence identifies Solomon as the best possible candidate for authorship. Many lay readers might question at this point why such an effort should even be expended to prove his authorship? It is stated simply in 1:1. So why all the fuss? Keep in mind two factors. There is a surprising number of "evangelical" scholars who have surrendered to higher criticism and do not view Solomonic authorship as being that important. Furthermore, even among evangelicals there is a problem with seeing Solomon as the hero because of his many wives and concubines that are clearly mentioned. Finally, since Solomon is *not* exactly the paragon of virtue, how could he write about his own less than heroic role? At this point, it is important again to attempt to locate the Song at some place within his life. That brings us to the vexing question of how we ought to interpret the Song of Songs? Is there a "story" beneath the poetry that it is attempting to relate?

## The Interpretation of the Song

The British OT scholar H. H. Rowley famously wrote this often-quoted judgment: "There is no book of the Old Testament which has found greater variety of interpretation than the Song of Songs" (Rowley, 197). Simply to spare the readers the many higher-critical and unbelieving evaluations of the song, we will focus on the interpretations of it by Jews and Christians who have a high view of it as canonical Hebrew and OT literature.

## Allegory

Because of the expressive statements about physical love in the book, some Jews and Christians—actually the majority in the last two thousand years—handle the love story as a grand allegory with very little attention given to any actual physical events it describes. Jewish allegorists see *Shulamit* as portraying Israel and *Shlomo* as portraying God. A.J. Rosenberg describes this approach as follows:

> Throughout Chapter One, Israel, represented by the woman, reminisces upon her early history, first going back to the giving of the Torah, symbolized by the kisses of the mouth, representing God's direct revelation of the Torah to Israel. Israel longs for this proximity to God as the deserted wife longs for the kisses of her husband who has forsaken her. (*The Five Megillot*, 17)

In this approach, it is not important to understand those breasts as literal, since they are an allegory for Moses and Aaron, and Israel is to lie between those two great individuals. This association of the "Beloved" with Israel's relationship with Yahweh, which was initiated with the deliverance from Egypt is why the book is read each year during Passover in Israel's religious festival cycle.

Christian allegorists, beginning with Origen in the third century, and continuing down to the present, view this book as describing Christ's dealings with His church. The chapter headings in the KJV indicate that the translators also viewed it as an allegory. The extremes to which an uncontrolled allegorical hermeneutic may go can be exemplified by the following "interpretations." The reference to *Shulamit* in 1:5 to being "black" means that the Church is black with sin but comely by conversion (Origen). The reference in 1:13 to being "between my breasts" refers to Old Testament and New Testament, between which is Christ (Cyril of Alexandria). The reference in 2:12 to "the voice of the turtledove heard in our land" refers to preaching of apostles (Cassiodorus). The reference to eating honey and drinking wine in 5:1 is a description of the Eucharist (many). Bernard of Clairvaux, author of the devotional hymn, "Jesus Thou Joy of Loving Hearts," wrote 78 sermons on the first 2 chapters of the book before he died, each of them following a detailed allegorical and Christological interpretation. Mercifully, dear Bernard passed on to glory before he could finish the rest of the book in this manner!

## Natural

Many contemporary scholars, desiring to distance themselves from both Jewish and Christian allegorical approaches to the Song of Songs, refuse to detect any kind of "story" being portrayed. Some authors just see a collection of lyrics expressing love. They acknowledge that Solomon and a Shulamite lass are mentioned, and occasionally will admit some sort of typical portrayal of Christ as Solomon and the Church as Shulamite. Evangelicals in this group would also see the Song as exemplifying and extolling married love while critics only detect a collection of Oriental love songs.

A brief evaluation of these approaches will now be offered before we approach the third "dramatic" approach which will be our main concern in the rest of the chapter. The greatest criticism of the Jewish and Christian allegorical treatments is the tremendous diversity that exists among the interpreters. Apart from Solomon being Christ and the Shulamite being the Church, the allegorical interpreters wander down all sorts of dead-end streets in their interpretations of the many details in the book. This criticism does not mean that symbolic applications to OT characters can never legitimately be made. One thinks of the dramatic details in the relationship between the prophet Hosea and his wayward wife Gomer (Hosea 1–3). While not discounting the actual events that transpired, the role of Hosea also visibly conveys Yahweh's love, even when it is severely tested. Gomer clearly represents Israel in their sinfulness. The intended symbolism (I prefer that word to allegory) is clear, especially when Yahweh and Israel are described that way so clearly in Hosea 3:1–5. With the Song, however, the details are not so obviously symbolic.

I will not comment on the critical approach to the Song because it doubts the book's inspiration and canonical role. The effort by many evangelical authors, however, to maintain some message about love and typology is also flawed. For example, what kind of example of married love is Solomon, with what we know of him outside the book (multiple wives and concubines in 1 Kings 11:3) and even inside the book (multiple wives and concubines in 6:8)? And the big question for evangelicals who advocate for a typological approach to the book also is evident. What sort of a type of Christ is Solomon?

## Dramatic

The third main approach to the book, while not discounting the important role of typology, is to see a drama being portrayed that can be detected in the obvious poetic language. This approach sees characters acting out their roles, which are described poetically. The first discerns two characters while the second approach, the one advocated in this book, sees three main characters.

**Solomon and Shulamite.** The popular *Unger's Bible Handbook* (299–300) describes this drama as follows. "King Solomon had a vineyard in the hill country of Ephraim, about 50 miles N of Jerusalem, 8:11. He let it out to keepers, 8:11, consisting of a mother, two sons, 1:6, and two daughters—the Shulamite, 6:13, and a little sister, 8:8. The Shulamite was 'the Cinderella' of the family, 1:5, naturally beautiful but unnoticed. Her brothers were likely half-brothers, 1:6. They made her work very hard tending the vineyards, so that she had little opportunity to care for her personal appearance, 1:6. She pruned the vines and set traps for the little foxes, 2:15. She also kept the flocks, 1:8. Being out in the open so much, she became sunburned, 1:5. One day a handsome stranger came to the vineyard. It was Solomon disguised. He showed an interest in her, and she became embarrassed concerning her personal appearance, 1:6. She took him for a shepherd and asked about his flocks, 1:7. He answered evasively, 1:8, but also spoke loving words to her, 1:8–10, and promised rich gifts for the future, 1:11. He won her heart and left with the promise that someday he would return. She dreamed of him at night and sometimes thought he was near, 3:1. Finally he did return in all his kingly splendor to make her his bride, 3:6–7. This prefigures Christ, who came first as Shepherd and won His Bride. Later He will return as King, and then will be consummated the marriage of the Lamb." The above summary conveys the approach that is probably espoused by many evangelical interpreters.

**Shlomo, Shulamit, and the Shepherd.** This is the approach to the book that is espoused in this commentary. What follows is a simple summary of the view, followed by a more detailed description with Scripture references of how I see the drama of the Song of Songs unfolding. The principal figure seems to be a Shulamite maiden who is transferred from a pastoral environment to the royal palace of Solomon. As the King woos this attractive country lass, his overtures are finally rejected. The splendor of the palace and the choral appeal of the court women fail to impress her. She passionately yearns for her former love. Ultimately her conflict is resolved as she declines the overtures of the king and returns to her shepherd hero. A more detailed summary, adapted from one of the most eloquent and scholarly advocates of the "The Three Character" view, Christian David Ginsburg, who first wrote about it in 1857. I have adapted his summary (Ginsburg, 4–6) by adding a few more modern expressions and the appropriate Scripture references to the events.

There was a family living at Shulam, consisting of a widowed mother, several sons, and one daughter, who maintained themselves by farming and shepherding. The brothers were particularly fond of their sister, and took her under their special care, promising that her wise behavior and virtue should be greatly rewarded by them (8:8–14). In the course of time, while tending the flock, and, according to the custom of the shepherds, resorting at noon beneath a tree for shelter against the mid-day sun, she met with a graceful shepherd youth to whom she afterward became betrothed (1:7; 2:16; 6:3). One morning in the Spring, this youth invited her to accompany him into the field, but the brothers overheard the invitation and anxious for the reputation of their sister, sent her to take care of the vineyards in order to prevent their meeting (2:15). The damsel, however, consoled her beloved and herself with the assurance that, though separated bodily, indissoluble ties existed between them over which her brothers had no control (2:16). She requested him to meet her in the evening (3:1) and when he did not come, she feared that some accident had happened to him on the way, so she went in search of him (3:2) and found him (3:4). The evening now was the only time in which they could enjoy each other's company, as during the day the damsel was occupied in the vineyards. On one occasion, when entering a garden, she accidentally came into the presence of King Solomon (6:11–12), who happened to be on a summer visit to that neighborhood (6:6–11). Struck with the beauty of the damsel, the King conducted her into his royal tent (1:2–4) and there, assisted by his court ladies (1:5–8), endeavored with alluring flatteries and promises, to gain her affections, but without effect (1:6–11). Released from the King's presence, the damsel sought an interview with her beloved shepherd (1:12–2:7). The King, however, took her to his capital in great pomp, in the hope of dazzling her with his splendor (3:6–11). But neither did this prevail because while even there she told her beloved shepherd, who had followed her to the capital (4:1–5), and obtained an interview with her, that she was anxious to leave the gaudy scene for her own home (4:6). The shepherd, on hearing this, praised her constancy (4:7–16), and such a manifestation of their mutual attachment took place, that several of the court-ladies were greatly affected by it (6:1). The King, still determined if possible to win her affection, watched for another favorable opportunity, and with flatteries and allurements, surpassing all that he had used before, tried to obtain his purpose (6:4–7:9). He promised to elevate her to the highest rank, and to raise her above his concubines and queens, if she would agree to his wishes. But faithful to her espousals, she refused all his overtures on the plea that her affections were pledged to another (7:10–8:4). The King, convinced at last that he could not possibly prevail, was obliged to dismiss her, and the shepherdess, in company with her beloved shepherd, returned to her native home (8:5–14). On their way home (8:5–7), they visited the tree under which they had first met, and there renewed their vows of faithfulness to each other. On her arrival in safety at her home, her brothers in accordance with the promise, rewarded her greatly for her virtuous conduct (8:8–9) accompanied (8:10–14) by a final reproval of Solomon.

## Evaluation of the Views

The next chapter will explain the Song of Songs in more detail, accompanied by a translation of the book for the convenience of the reader. The conclusion to this chapter is a brief criticism of the traditional two-character view.

Evangelical advocates of a two-character approach must face some serious questions. These include the following. (1) What kind of example was Solomon of "pure married love" in light of 1 Kings 11:1–8? If Solomon is honestly not such an example, why should this book merit any consideration at all as being worthy of a place in the canonical literature called the Old Testament? (2) An honest reading of what could be called the "epilogue" (Song 8:10–14) places Solomon in a bad light and the immediately preceding passage, which all see as the message of the book, portrays love as triumphing over a severe test of its reality (8:6–7). In other words, if love survived the flood of "many waters" then it must have been put to the test. And in the immediate context it is Solomon who provided that test (8:11–12). (3) It has already been mentioned that if an attempt is made in the two-character approach to make Solomon a type, we should be terribly embarrassed to offer the son of David as in any way a type of our Messiah! (4) One of the biggest arguments for the three-character view is the presence in the narrative quite early on of someone displaying "shepherd" characteristics (1:7–8). The attempt by some to suggest that Solomon is disguising himself as a shepherd totally disregards the need for this powerful king to disguise himself, and also exemplifies a terrible strain by the advocates of a two-character view to explain this character away.

More will be said in defense of the "Three Character" view, namely *Shlomo, Shulamit* and the Shepherd, in the next chapter. To end this chapter, I want to address the possible objection about the novelty of this view. In other words, is it the creation of the author or at least part of a minority of interpreters of the Song. Consider the following evidence. Although the "traditional" Jewish approach to the book is that its two characters, *Shlomo* and *Shulamit*, are allegorical figures of Yahweh and Israel, rabbinical advocates of three characters include the revered Abraham ibn Ezra and the 13th-century Ibn Caspi and Moshe Ibn Tibbon. Modern Jewish writers affirming the three-character view are the German Max Brod (ca. 1921) and the more contemporary Chaim Rabin (1973).

Christian writers who have proposed and defended this approach include the following: J. Jacobi (1771); Christian David Ginsburg (1857); Frederic Godet (1894); William Griffis (1889), E.W. Bullinger (1920); W. Twyman Williams (1947); Graham Scroggie (1958); J. Barton Payne (1965); Fred Afman (1966); Samuel Schultz (1968); Arthur G. Clarke (1970); Walter Kaiser (1979; 2000); John Phillips (1984); Hill and Walton (1991); Larry Helyer (1996); Iain Provan (2001); and Miles Van Pelt (2016). This extensive list is not an effort to settle this issue by a popular vote! These scholarly writers simply provide evidence that the view, although sometimes ridiculed as extreme, is not novel and weird, but an interpretation that has been espoused by solid scholars. This view vindicates the literal interpretation of Scripture and enjoys the privilege of spiritual application within the limits of Biblical history. This approach will prevent excessive allegorizing because many passages will be allowed their historical significance and no more.

Finally, in this approach the spiritual value of the book is also enhanced. The faithfulness of the Shulamite illustrates the power and purity of marital love and is typical of the believer's faithfulness to Christ in the midst of temptation. It is the Shepherd who typifies Christ, *not* Solomon. The message of the book is a challenge to loyalty and fidelity to the "One who loved us and gave Himself for us" and to stand fast in our lives and loyalty to Him, in the face of the fiercest temptations and severest trials.

## Further Reading

An important article about the Song is "The Interpretation of the Song of Songs" by H. H. Rowley in *The Servant of the Lord and Other Essays on the Old Testament, 2nd rev. (Blackwell, 1965)*, 197–245. I have mentioned in the chapter over a dozen authors who advocate a three-character approach to the book, namely, Shlomo, Shulamit, and the Shepherd. A difficult volume to find is the scholarly defense by the Hebrew-Christian scholar C. D. Ginsburg, originally published in 1857 and reissued as *The Song of Songs and Cohelet*, ed. Harry Orlinsky (Ktav Publishing House, 1970), 1–191. While many of the other books are out of print, the reader can find a full commentary from this viewpoint by Iain Provan in *Ecclesiastes, Song of Songs*, as part of the NIV Application Commentary (Zondervan, 2001). Another scholarly defense is in *A Biblical-Theological Introduction to the Old Testament*, ed. Miles Van Pelt (also the author of that section), Crossway, 2016, 419–456.

# 4

# A Translation of the Song of Songs

## One Approach to the Text and the Speakers

Before we look closer at a translation of the Song, it is helpful to see some specific examples of the three-character view. J. Barton Payne in his *Theology of the Older Testament* (523) offered the following helpful analysis of the text. His proposal is that the Shulamite was Abishag the Shunammite who was brought from her Galilee village to be David's non-sexual companion in old age (1 Kings 1:3–4). While I am not convinced that the Shulamite was Abishag, his suggestion about the possible identification of the speakers is worth considering. The value of the following reconstruction of the action and "speeches" in the book is significant because it is simply difficult to discern clearly who is being addressed and who is speaking in the book. The way that Hebrew often indicates the gender of the verb's person helps at times because we can conclude that a male or a female is speaking. Furthermore, the context also speaks of the daughters of Jerusalem and the brothers of *Shulamit*. As you read the Biblical text which follows this analysis, this reconstruction can be helpful to guide your reading.

Act I. **SHULAMIT'S PLIGHT** (1:3–5). Setting: "The city" (Jerusalem, 3:3), the palace chambers (1:4; 2:9).
    Scene 1 (1:2–7)
        Daughters of Jerusalem: (2–4) Rightly do we all love Solomon.
        Shulamit: (5–7) describes herself: But I love a shepherd.

Daughters: (8) You can have him! (enter Solomon)
Solomon: (9–11) praises her
Shulamit: (12–14) I have a plant in my bosom reminding me of my shepherd.
Solomon: (15) praise
Shulamit: (16–2:1) My beloved is the fair one; I'm a country flower.
Solomon: (2) You are a lily among thorns (reflects on the harem).
Shulamit: (3–7) Shepherd's banner over me was love (5, overcome with love, not sick of it).
   **The charge**: Don't force love.
Scene 2 (2:8–3:5), reveries.
Shulamit: (8–9) I can hear him saying:
Shepherd: (10–14) Come to me (a highpoint in poetic expression).
Shulamit: (15–17) Stop the foxes first? But why worry, it's love!
(3:1–5) second reverie, finding him and marriage.
   **The charge**: Don't force love.

Act II. **SHULAMIT'S STEADFASTNESS** (3:6–8:4). Setting: Galilee? (4:8), a royal scene (6).
Scene 1 (3:6–5:1)
Daughters #1: (6) What comes?
Daughters #2: (7–11) Solomon in chariot, ready for his wedding.
Solomon: (4:1–5) praises Shulamit
Shulamit: (6) I would rather be home.
Solomon: (7–15) Come with me, my heart is ravished.
Shulamit: (16) May I be worthy of my Shepherd, whose I am.
Solomon: (5:1) But here I am, let's drink.
Scene 2 (5:2–6:3), dream told the daughters
Shulamit: (2–8) I dreamed I missed him; if you see him tell him I am true.
Daughters: (9) Who is this man, anyhow?

Shulamit: (10–16) He's the fairest of 10,000, altogether lovely.

Daughters: (6:1) We are interested.

Shulamit: (2–3) Oh no, I am his and he is mine.

Scene 3 (6:4–8:4)

Solomon: (4–9) You dismay me, better than 60 queens and 80 concubines.

Daughters: (10) (insulted) What are you saying!

Shulamit: (11–12) I was summoned to court; I came not by my own will.

Daughters: (13a) Good, let us see you.

Shulamit: (13b) I'm no public dancer.

Solomon: (7:1–9a) praise; ends, "Thy mouth is like the best wine—"

He may have been building up to a kiss and she breaks in.

Shulamit: (9b–8:4) "reserved for my Shepherd. I am his."

She calls for her Shepherd to come and get her.

**The charge.** Don't force love.

Act III. **SHULAMIT'S REWARD** (8:5–14). Setting: Her home in Galilee.

Only scene:

Brothers: (5a) Who comes with her beloved?

Shepherd: (5b) points out "apple tree" where they fell in love, and her cottage

Shulamit: (6–7; the climactic statement), Love conquers all, a flame of Yahweh.

Brothers: (8) When she was young, what did we warn her?

(9) A firm, chaste wall, rewarded; a yielding door, no.

Shulamit: (10–12) I proved a wall before Solomon. He can have his wealth: I have my "vineyard."

Shepherd: (13) Say that to me.

Shulamit: (14) Make haste, my beloved

## The Actual Translation

Too often a commentary on a Biblical book is not accompanied by the very text that is being studied. It is not enough to assume the readers are familiar with the Song of Songs. Furthermore, translations like the King James Version often preserve chapter headings that portray allegorical views. Therefore, we include the entire text of the book adapted from the *Legacy Standard Bible*. In the Biblical text I have inserted before each speech the suggested identity of the speaker in the Hebrew form of their names, *Shulamit* and *Shlomo*. I have also bolded the three occurrences of the "charge" since each time it also serves to introduce the arrival on stage of a new character. This will be helpful when we look at another literary analysis that follows the translation. Enjoy your reading! "Open our eyes Lord, that we may see wonderful things in your word."

### Chapter One

1 The Song of Songs, which is Solomon's.

**DAUGHTERS**
2 "May he kiss me with the kisses of his mouth!
For your love is better than wine.
3 Your oils have a pleasing fragrance,
Your name is *like* purified oil;
Therefore the maidens love you.
4 Draw me after you *and* let us run *together*!
The king has brought me into his chambers."
"We will rejoice in you and be glad;
We will extol your love more than wine.
Rightly do they love you."

**SHULAMIT**
5 "I am black but lovely,
O daughters of Jerusalem,
Like the tents of Kedar,
Like the curtains of Solomon.

6 Do not look at me because I am swarthy,
For the sun has burned me.
My mother's sons were angry with me;
They made me caretaker of the vineyards,
*But* I have not taken care of my own vineyard.
7 Tell me, O you whom my soul loves,
Where do you shepherd *your flock*,
Where do you make *it* lie down at noon?
For why should I be like one who veils herself
Beside the flocks of your companions?"

**DAUGHTERS**
8 "If you yourself do not know,
Most beautiful among women,
Go forth on the trail of the flock
And pasture your young goats
By the dwellings of the shepherds.

**SHLOMO**
9 "To a mare of mine among the chariots of Pharaoh
I compare you, O my darling.
10 Your cheeks are lovely with ornaments,
Your neck with strings of beads."
11 "We will make for you ornaments of gold
With beads of silver."

**SHULAMIT**
12 "While the king was at his banqueting table,
My perfume gave forth its fragrance.
13 My beloved is to me a pouch of myrrh
Which lies all night between my breasts.
14 My beloved is to me a cluster of henna blossoms
In the vineyards of Engedi."

**SHLOMO**
15 "Behold, you are beautiful, my darling,
Behold, you are beautiful!

Your eyes are *like* doves."

**SHULAMIT**
**16** "Behold, you are handsome, my beloved,
Indeed, *so* pleasant!
Indeed, our couch is luxuriant!
17 The beams of our houses are cedars,
Our rafters, cypresses."

## Chapter Two

1 "I am the rose of Sharon,
The lily of the valleys."

**SHLOMO**
2 "Like a lily among the thorns,
So is my darling among the daughters."

**SHULAMIT**
3 "Like an apple tree among the trees of the forest,
So is my beloved among the sons.
In his shade I had great desire and sat down,
And his fruit was sweet to my taste.
4 He has brought me to *his* house of banqueting,
And his banner over me is love.
5 Sustain me with raisin cakes,
Refresh me with apples,
Because I am lovesick.
6 Let his left hand be under my head
And his right hand embrace me."

**7 "I call you to *solemnly* swear, O daughters of Jerusalem,
By the gazelles or by the hinds of the field,
That you do not arouse or awaken *my* love
Until she pleases."**

# A Translation of the Song of Songs

**SHULAMIT**
8 "The voice of my beloved!
Behold, he is coming,
Leaping on the mountains,
Jumping on the hills!
9 My beloved is like a gazelle or a young stag.
Behold, he is standing behind our wall;
He gazes through the windows;
He is peering through the lattice.

**SHEPHERD**
10 "My beloved answered and said to me,
'Arise, my darling, my beautiful one,
And come along.
11 For behold, the winter is past,
The rain is over; it is gone.
12 The flowers have appeared in the land;
The time for pruning has arrived;
And the voice of the turtledove has been heard in our land.
13 The fig tree has ripened its figs,
And the vines in blossom have given forth *their* fragrance.
Arise, my darling, my beautiful one,
And come along!'"

14 "O my dove, in the clefts of the rock,
In the secret place of the steep pathway,
Let me see your appearance,
Let me hear your voice;
For your voice is sweet,
And your appearance is lovely."

**SHULAMIT**
15 "Seize the foxes for us,
The little foxes that are wreaking destruction on the vineyards,
While our vineyards are in blossom."

16 "My beloved is mine, and I am his,

He who shepherds *his flock* among the lilies.
17 Until the day breathes and the shadows flee,
Turn, my beloved, and be like a gazelle
Or a young stag on the mountains of Bether."

## Chapter Three

1 "On my bed night after night I sought him
Whom my soul loves;
I sought him but did not find him.
2 'I must arise now and go about the city;
In the streets and in the squares
I must seek him whom my soul loves.'
I sought him but did not find him.
3 The watchmen who go about the city found me,
*And I said*, 'Have you seen him whom my soul loves?'
4 Scarcely had I passed them by
When I found him whom my soul loves;
I seized him and would not let him go
Until I had brought him to my mother's house,
And into the chamber of her who conceived me."

**5 "I call you to *solemnly* swear, O daughters of Jerusalem,
By the gazelles or by the hinds of the field,
That you do not arouse or awaken *my* love
Until she pleases."**

**DAUGHTERS**
6 "Who is this coming up from the wilderness
Like columns of smoke,
As rising incense of myrrh and frankincense,
With all scented powders of the merchant?
7 Behold, it is the *traveling* couch of Solomon;
Sixty mighty men around it,
Of the mighty men of Israel.
8 All of them are those who seize the sword,
Learned in war;

Each man has his sword at his side,
*Guarding* against the dreadful things of the night.
9 King Solomon has made for himself a sedan chair
From the timber of Lebanon.
10 He made its posts of silver,
Its back of gold
*And* its seat of purple fabric,
*With* its interior inlaid with love
By the daughters of Jerusalem.
11 Go forth and see, O daughters of Zion,
King Solomon with the crown
With which his mother has crowned him
On the day of his wedding,
And on the day of his gladness of heart."

## Chapter Four

**SHLOMO**
1 "Behold, you are beautiful, my darling,
Behold, you are beautiful!
Your eyes are *like* doves behind your veil;
Your hair is like a flock of goats
That have leapt down from Mount Gilead.
2 Your teeth are like a flock of *newly* shorn ewes
Which have come up from *their* washing,
All of which bear twins,
And not one among them has lost her young.
3 Your lips are like a scarlet thread,
And your mouth is lovely.
Your temples are like a slice of a pomegranate
Behind your veil.
4 Your neck is like the tower of David,
Built with rows of stones
On which are hung one thousand shields,
All the small shields of the mighty men.
5 Your two breasts are like two fawns,
Twins of a gazelle

Which feed among the lilies.

**SHULAMIT**
6 Until the day breathes
And the shadows flee,
I will go my way to the mountain of myrrh
And to the hill of frankincense.

**SHLOMO**
7 "You are altogether beautiful, my darling,
And there is no blemish in you.
8 *Come* with me from Lebanon, *my* bride,
May you come with me from Lebanon.
Journey down from the top of Amana,
From the top of Senir and Hermon,
From the dens of lions,
From the mountains of leopards.
9 You have made my heart beat faster, my sister, *my* bride;
You have made my heart beat faster with a single *glance* of your eyes,
With a single strand of your necklace.
10 How beautiful is your love, my sister, *my* bride!
How much better is your love than wine,
And the fragrance of your oils
Than all *kinds* of spices!
11 Your lips, *my* bride, drip honey from the comb;
Honey and milk are under your tongue,
And the fragrance of your garments is like the fragrance of Lebanon.
12 A garden locked is my sister, *my* bride,
A rock garden locked, a spring sealed up.
13 Your shoots are an orchard of pomegranates
With choice fruits, henna with nard plants,
14 Nard and saffron, calamus and cinnamon,
With all the trees of frankincense,
Myrrh and aloes, along with all the finest spices.
15 *You are* a garden spring,

A well of fresh water,
And streams *flowing* from Lebanon."

**SHULAMIT**
16 "Awake, O north *wind*,
And come, *wind of* the south;
Make my garden breathe out *fragrance*,
Let its spices flow forth.
May my beloved come into his garden
And eat its choice fruits!"

## Chapter Five

**SHLOMO**
1 "I have come into my garden, my sister, *my* bride;
I have picked my myrrh along with my balsam.
I have eaten my honeycomb with my honey;
I have drunk my wine with my milk.
Eat, friends;
Drink and imbibe deeply, O lovers."

**SHULAMIT**
2 "I was asleep, but my heart was awake.
A voice! My beloved was knocking:
'Open to me, my sister, my darling,
My dove, my perfect one!
For my head is full of dew,
My locks with the damp of the night.'
3 I have taken off my longsleeved garment,
How can I put it on *again*?
I have washed my feet,
How can I dirty them *again*?
4 My beloved sent forth his hand through the opening,
And my feelings moaned for him.
5 I arose to open to my beloved;
And my hands dripped with myrrh,

And my fingers with liquid myrrh,
On the handles of the lock.
6 I opened to my beloved,
But my beloved had turned away *and* passed by!
My soul went out *to him* as he spoke.
I searched for him, but I did not find him;
I called him, but he did not answer me.
7 The watchmen who go about in the city found me,
They struck me *and* wounded me;
The guardsmen of the walls took away my shawl from me.
8 I call you to *solemnly* swear, O daughters of Jerusalem,
If you find my beloved,
What will you tell him?
*Tell him* that I am sick with love."

## DAUGHTERS
**9** "What is your beloved *that he is* more than *any other* beloved,
O most beautiful among women?
What is your beloved *that he is* more than *any other* beloved,
That thus you call us to *solemnly* swear?"

## SHULAMIT
**10** "My beloved is dazzling and ruddy,
Lifted up as a banner among ten thousand.
11 His head is *like* gold, fine gold;
His locks are *like* clusters of dates
*And* black as a raven.
12 His eyes are like doves
Beside streams of water,
Washed in milk,
*And* sitting in *their* setting.
13 His cheeks are like a bed of spices,
Towers of sweetscented herbs;
His lips are lilies
Dripping with liquid myrrh.
14 His hands are rods of gold
Set with beryl;

His abdomen is a plate of ivory
Inlaid with sapphires.
15 His legs are pillars of marble
Set on bases of fine gold;
His appearance is like Lebanon
Choice as the cedars.
16 His mouth is *full of* sweetness.
And he is wholly desirable.
This is my beloved and this is my friend,
O daughters of Jerusalem."

## Chapter Six

**DAUGHTERS**
1 "Where has your beloved gone,
O most beautiful among women?
Where has your beloved turned,
That we may seek him with you?"

**SHULAMIT**
2 "My beloved has gone down to his garden,
To the beds of spices,
To shepherd *his flock* in the gardens
And gather lilies.
3 I am my beloved's and my beloved is mine,
He who shepherds *his flock* among the lilies."

**SHLOMO**
4 "You are as beautiful as Tirzah, my darling,
As lovely as Jerusalem,
As majestic as an army with banners.
5 Turn your eyes away from me,
For they have overwhelmed me;
Your hair is like a flock of goats
That have leapt down from Gilead.
6 Your teeth are like a flock of ewes
Which have come up from *their* washing,

All of which bear twins,
And not one among them has lost her young.
7 Your temples are like a slice of a pomegranate
Behind your veil.
8 There are sixty queens and eighty concubines,
And maidens without number;
9 She is the only one—my dove, my perfect one;
She is the only one of her mother;
She is the pure one of her who bore her.
The daughters saw her and called her blessed,
The queens and the concubines *also*, and they praised her, *saying*,

**DAUGHTERS**
10 'Who is this that looks down like the dawn,
As beautiful as the full moon,
As pure as the sun,
As majestic as an army with banners?'

**SHULAMIT**
11 I went down to the garden of nut trees
To see the blossoms of the valley,
To see whether the vine had flourished
*Or* the pomegranates had bloomed.
12 I did not know *it, but* my soul set me
*Among* the chariots of my noble people."

**DAUGHTERS**
13 "Come back, come back, O Shulammite;
Come back, come back, that we may behold you!"

**SHULAMIT**
"Why should you behold the Shulammite,
As at the dance of the two companies?

## Chapter Seven

**SHLOMO**
1 "How beautiful are your feet in sandals,
O noble's daughter!
The curves of your thighs are like ornaments,
The work of the hands of an artist.
2 Your navel is *like* a round basin
Which never lacks mixed wine;
Your belly is like a heap of wheat
Encircled with lilies.
3 Your two breasts are like two fawns,
Twins of a gazelle.
4 Your neck is like a tower of ivory,
Your eyes *like* the pools in Heshbon
By the gate of Bathrabbim;
Your nose is like the tower of Lebanon,
Which faces toward Damascus.
5 Your head crowns you like Carmel,
And the flowing locks of your head are like purple threads;
*The* king is captivated by *your* tresses.
6 How beautiful and how pleasant you are,
*My* love, with *all* your pleasures!
7 Your stature is like a palm tree,
And your breasts are *like its* clusters.
8 I said, 'I will climb the palm tree;
I will seize its fruit stalks.'
Oh, may your breasts be like clusters of the vine,
And the fragrance of your breath like apples,
9 And your mouth like the best wine!"

**SHULAMIT**
"It goes *down* smoothly for my beloved,
Flowing gently *through* the lips of those who fall asleep.
10 "I am my beloved's,
And his desire is for me.
11 Come, my beloved, let us go out into the fields,

Let us spend the night in the villages.
12 Let us rise early *and go* to the vineyards;
Let us see whether the vine has flourished
*And its* blossoms have opened,
*And whether* the pomegranates have bloomed.
There I will give you my love.
13 The mandrakes have given forth fragrance;
And over our doors are all choice *fruits*,
Both new and old,
Which I have treasured up for you, my beloved.

## Chapter Eight

1 "Oh that you were like a brother to me
Who nursed at my mother's breasts.
*If* I found you outside, I would kiss you;
No one would despise me, either.
2 I would lead you *and* bring you
Into the house of my mother, who used to teach me;
I would give you spiced wine to drink from the sweet wine of my pomegranates.
3 Let his left hand be under my head
And his right hand embrace me."

**4 "I call you to *solemnly* swear, O daughters of Jerusalem,
Why should you arouse or awaken *my* love
Until she pleases?"**

### BROTHERS
5 "Who is this coming up from the wilderness
Leaning on her beloved?"

### SHEPHERD
"Beneath the apple tree I awakened you;
There your mother was in labor with you;
There she was in labor *and* gave you birth.

## SHULAMIT

6 Put me like a seal over your heart,
Like a seal on your arm.
For love is as strong as death,
Jealousy is as severe as Sheol;
Its flashes are flashes of fire,
The *very* flame of Yah.
7 Many waters cannot quench love,
Nor will rivers overflow it;
If a man were to give all the riches of his house for love,
It would be utterly despised."

## BROTHERS

8 "We have a little sister,
And she has no breasts;
What shall we do for our sister
On the day when she is spoken for?
9 If she is a wall,
We will build on her a battlement of silver;
But if she is a door,
We will barricade her with planks of cedar."

## SHULAMIT

10 "I was a wall, and my breasts were like towers;
Then I became in his eyes as one who finds peace.
11 Solomon had a vineyard at Baalhamon;
He gave the vineyard to caretakers.
Each one was to bring one thousand *shekels* of silver for its fruit.
12 My very own vineyard is before me;
The thousand *shekels* are for you, Solomon,
And two hundred are for those who take care of its fruit."

## SHEPHERD

13 "O you who sit in the gardens,
*My* companions are giving heed to your voice—
Let me hear it!"

**SHULAMIT**
14 "Hurry, my beloved,
And be like a gazelle or a young stag
On the mountains of spices."

NOTE: The reader should know that every detail of this analysis may not always compel agreement. Anyone who has worked through this amazing text knows that at times it is difficult to be dogmatic about who is speaking and whom is being addressed. But even if we have not isolated exactly the identity of each speaker in very instance, the above is an approximate effort that still supports the three-character approach to the song. Finally, the translation in 2:7; 3:5; and 8:4 to not "awake my love until she pleases" reflects the feminine subject of the verb. It is also possible to translate the verb "until it pleases" referring to love since that noun is feminine in gender.

## A Literary Approach to the Book

A contemporary scholar, Miles Van Pelt, has also offered a scholarly defense of the three character view, while also noting the previously mentioned and thrice-repeated "charge" as a literary hinge in both the text and the story. The Hebrew reads three times in 2:7; 3:5, and 8:4: "I call you to solemnly swear..." In each of the three occurrences this oath or charge is followed by the announcement of an individual's arrival such as "Behold he is coming" (2:8). This oath thus marks the end of a major section and the announcement of an arrival that marks the beginning of a new section. Van Pelt has thus enlisted the linguistic principles of discourse analysis in his analysis. The four main divisions of the Song are as follows, utilizing the Hebrew names of the two named characters.

I. The Temptations of *Shlomo*'s Harem (1:2–2:7)
II. The Arrival of the Shepherd (2:8–3:5)
III. The Arrival of *Shlomo* (3:6–8:4)
IV. The Arrival of *Shulamit* (8:5–14)

The reader is invited at this point to follow this outline and read again the text of the Song in the preceding Biblical text. All readers are advised as well that no scholars may be absolutely dogmatic that they have figured out every nuance of every speaker. However, that is true no matter what approach we take to the various characters in the book! In my opinion this is the best way to read this poetic text. In this analysis, the Song of Songs is a poetic wisdom song that celebrates the subject of marriage and love from the perspective of a young woman. This perspective is probably unique among the texts of all the canonical books and should offer encouragement to modern readers of any gender, but especially to female readers.

A few pointers to readers as they work through the text that justifies the proposed number of characters. The arrival of the male figure, the Shepherd in 2:8–14, indicates that he does not have access to the Shulamite, since there is a "wall" keeping them apart so he can only search for her through "the lattice." By way of contrast, Solomon's arrival in 3:6 indicates that he has full access at that point. This reality explains her later rejection of Solomon and the harem life in 8:11–12, but her presence with the Shepherd in 8:5.

On a broader scale, but in harmony with a Biblical theological approach to the Solomonic books, the Solomon figure portrays not the way of wisdom but the way of folly which is evil in the Lord's eyes (1 Kings 11:1–6). This also parallels the wisdom instruction in what Solomon himself had earlier written in Proverbs 1–9. The instruction embodied in Lady Wisdom in Prov 5:15–20, for example, shares language and imagery with Song of Songs 3:13–18 and 4:6–9. The reader is invited to examine the texts to see these remarkable parallels, even though we will recognize that Solomon is not following the principles that he had written in Proverbs earlier in his life!

The instruction in the Song is also similar to the contrasting description of Lady Folly in Prov 7:4–27. Thus a lady (in this case) is challenged to choose between two men, the allurement of one that leads to death and the attractions of another that leads to life. The conclusion is that the instruction embodied in the poetry of the Song intends to teach young women to choose a husband wisely and thus resist the deadly temptation of folly symbolized by

Solomon with the offers of wealth and ease and prestige and security, at least for the present (Van Pelt, 433–436)!

## Locating the Song of Songs in the Life of Solomon

The neglect and the misuse of Yahweh's gifts by Solomon brought the need for some spiritual conviction. Warned by David as he became king and by Yahweh during the building of the temple, Solomon enjoyed the blessing of God during the early years of his reign. The completion of his buildings, which marked the middle of his reign, brought a second vision of warning from Yahweh, but the middle-aged king was becoming self-sufficient, still religious but also taking liberties with the instructions and warnings of the Torah. His subsequent multiplication of wealth, horses from Egypt, and wives demonstrated the need for this conviction, but even the expression of God's displeasure through the prophet brought no change, because foreign women had turned his heart away from Yahweh. It is in the middle section of his reign that we best locate the setting for the Song.

The Song of Songs, therefore, is the record of the conviction that God used to reclaim his king. The book claims Solomon as its author, as the opening verse claims the Song as his best. The interpretation by the two-character method is not acceptable because it presents no real conflict, and the allegorical approach leads to excesses with interpreter becoming their own guide. The three-character approach is adopted because it adheres to a literal-historical basis with the opportunity for spiritual application, which all inspired Scripture possesses. The Shulamite defends herself from the temptations offered by the world represented by Solomon. By her testimony that love is a divine gift that no one may stir it up, she declares her devotion for the Shepherd, who can validly typify Christ. She desires to be with him despite the temptations of the palace, and finally delights in her marriage to that Shepherd. He has shown respect for her, responded to her needs, and resolved to honor their God-given love. Solomon reveals himself, however, as a proud and powerful suitor, who seeks by praise to break down her resistance, but must pause in respect as he simply cannot stand before her eyes of purity.

In frustration he gives voice to his passions, but the Shulamite withstands his temptations and with the king's permission triumphantly returns to her Shepherd, happy to keep her own vineyard.

The silence of Solomon after the Shulamite's departure and the fact that this book is written by Solomon's inspired pen gives it a spiritual purpose worthy of inclusion in the canon. This purpose was to extol the truth and the beauty of Yahweh's gift of love exemplified by the Shulamite and her Shepherd. It could also reveal the shame of Solomon, stunning him into conviction for his gross sin of having turned his heart from God through the rebukes administered to him by the Shulamite. The misuse of his divine gifts of wisdom and wealth to build temples for the gods of his many wives was also rebuked. The record of this convicting experience would prepare also for the confessions of Ecclesiastes and the restoration of the once noble and spiritual Solomon. (My thanks to my first OT mentor, Fred Afman, for suggesting some of these final reflections in his unpublished dissertation.)

### A Personal Observation

Helen and I have the following verse references from the Song of Songs engraved inside our wedding rings. These truths have kept our marriage intact through some severe tests and trials now for over fifty-one years. Allow me to quote the verses and offer a simple outline of their contents. Readers can then apply these truths to their own marriages or to their future "Shulamite," "*Shlomo*," or Shepherd, whoever that may be. I have probably delivered over a dozen messages from this text at weddings as I faced a happy but nervous couple.

> Song 8:6–7:
> "Put me like a seal over your heart,
> Like a seal on your arm.
> For love is as strong as death,
> Jealousy is as severe as Sheol;
> Its flashes are flashes of fire,
> The *very* flame of Yah.

Many waters cannot quench love,
Nor will rivers overflow it;
If a man were to give all the riches of his house for love,
It would be utterly despised."

Four affirmations about true love can be drawn from this text.

1. Love is **Permanent** ("seal")
2. Love is **Powerful** ("vehement flame" or "the flame of Yah")
3. Love is **Persevering** ("many waters")
4. Love is **Priceless** ("all one's riches...condemned")

Today a circular ring portrays the endless character that we desire for our marriages. In ancient times such permanency was conveyed by the symbol of a **seal**. Contrary to the way matrimony has often developed and been portrayed in modern days, marriages are not made to be broken. Shulamit's pledge to her Shepherd included a permanent commitment. Marriages today demand no less a commitment. One of the most powerful forces in the world is a real marriage relationship between a man and woman. It is so powerful that she chose to describe it through the metaphor of fire. But this love is not just something conjured up by two people. Love is of God and that is why it is described as Yah's **flame**. The two Hebrew letters added to the word flame (*shalhevetyah*) is the same abbreviated "Yahweh" added to the well-known Hebrew word "Hallelu-**yah**." That combination means "praise Yahweh" and this addition means the "flame of Yahweh." Recognizing this poetic signature of Israel's Deity also puts the lie to the charge that God is nowhere mentioned in this book. Furthermore, if true love is **permanent** and **powerful**, then it will **persevere** no matter who or what opposes it. A rival powerfully desired to drown Shulamit's love by his wealth and power, but her fiery love for her Shepherd could not be extinguished by any flood of waters brought against it. Finally, love cannot be bought with a price because it is simply **priceless**. The popular song states "can't buy me love." If that is true about secular love, how much more does the wealth of a powerful king fail to secure what only Yahweh can provide: a permanent and powerful and persevering and priceless love.

The final comment offered here on the Song of Songs is that in light of this precious passage crowning the last chapter, it again is evidence, as we have said before, that the key to the house of this amazing literary treasure is near the back door!

# 5

# Ecclesiastes or the *Kohelet*

## Introduction

Sometimes a passage from the Bible shows up in unexpected places. Consider the following lyrics of a popular song in the past.

To everything (turn, turn, turn)
There is a season (turn, turn, turn)
And a time to every purpose under heaven.

A time to be born, a time to die,
A time to plant, a time to reap,
A time to kill, a time to heal,
A time to laugh, a time to weep.

To everything (turn, turn, turn)
There is a season (turn, turn, turn)
And a time to every purpose under heaven.

A time to build up, a time to break down,
A time to dance, a time to mourn,
A time to cast away stones, a time to gather stones together.

To everything (turn, turn, turn)
There is a season (turn, turn, turn)
And a time to every purpose, under heaven.

A time of love, a time of hate,
A time of war, a time of peace,
A time you may embrace, a time to refrain from embracing,

To everything (turn, turn, turn)
There is a season (turn, turn, turn)
And a time to every purpose under heaven.

A time to gain, a time to lose,
A time to rend, a time to sew,
A time for love, a time for hate,
A time for peace, I swear it's not too late.

This song is titled "Turn, Turn, Turn" (not surprisingly), and was performed by the Byrds with the music written by Pete Seeger. Years after its popularity it was voted the top single folk-rock song of the 1960's. What is fascinating for our purposes is that apart from that repeating refrain and the final line, the lyrics are drawn entirely from Ecclesiastes 3:1–8!

Quotations from the book before us in this chapter often are heard, even among those who are not necessarily avid Bible readers. The familiar expression echoed often in the book, "vanity of vanities, all is vanity," has appeared as an answer on the game show, Jeopardy, with the correct question being "What is Ecclesiastes?" We will see that the word by itself ("vanity") appears an additional twenty-seven times in the book! Passages in this book about the hopelessness of life are often quoted by skeptics. Watchtower members have often quoted Ecclesiastes 9:5 to "prove" that the Bible teaches that there is no life after death. That verse reads: "For the living know they will die; but the dead do not know anything, nor have they any longer a reward, for the memory of them is forgotten."

On the other hand, many Christian youth groups have often heard the following exhortation quoted to them: "Remember also your Creator in the days of your youth" (12:1a). And the final admonition in the book is often quoted as an admonition for everyone: "The end of the matter, all *that* has been heard: fear God and keep His commandments."

And yet there are some who charge that since this book is not quoted in the New Testament, why should we bother with it? Actually, this may not be strictly the case. Paul's remark that we brought nothing into this world and it is certain we will take nothing out (1 Tim 6:7) could be an explicit use of a verse such as "All go to the same place. All came from the dust, and all return to the dust" (3:20). More on the subject of Ecclesiastes and the New Testament will appear the next chapter.

So what do we make of a book in the Bible that contains these and other profound thoughts alongside other statements that can often shock believers that such things are even in the Bible? I believe that there is a key that unlocks the presence of both these apparently extreme viewpoints and offers a way to appreciate this book in a fresh way. But in this chapter we must first lay out some introductory matters that will provide the context for that key which, not surprisingly, is also found near the "back door" of the book.

## The Title

Here are some ways that popular English versions have handled the translation of *Kohelet* קֹהֶלֶת in 1:1:

LSB: The words of the **Preacher**, the son of David, king in Jerusalem.

NAU The words of the **Preacher**, the son of David, king in Jerusalem.

NKJ The words of the **Preacher**, the son of David, king in Jerusalem.

KJV The words of the **Preacher**, the son of David, king in Jerusalem

ESV: The words of the **Preacher**, the son of David, king in Jerusalem.

NRS: The words of the **Teacher**, the son of David, king in Jerusalem.

NIV: The words of the **Teacher**, son of David, king in Jerusalem:

NET: The words of the **Teacher**, the son of David, king in Jerusalem:

CSB: The words of the **Teacher**, son of David, king in Jerusalem.

CEB: The words of the **Teacher** of the Assembly, David's son, king in Jerusalem.

NLT: These are the words of the **Teacher**, King David's son, who ruled in Jerusalem.

Douay: The words of **Ecclesiastes**, the son of David, king of Jerusalem.

While the KJV rendered the word as "Preacher," the traditional title of the book, Ecclesiastes, looks like it came from the Douay Version, the R.C. translation of the Vulgate. It also reflects the LXX translation Ἐκκλησιαστης.

As one can see, the title which is most familiar to us, Ecclesiastes, actually comes from the Greek translation of the Hebrew title in the Septuagint. The word *ekklesia* means "gathering" or "congregation" and is often translated as "church" in the New Testament. With the added suffix -stes that indicates the actor of the root word, it would refer to the one who leads the *ecclesia*.

The Hebrew word under this translation is *Kohelet*, and I often refer to the book simply by its title of *Kohelet*. The word is a feminine participle of a verb that means "to assemble" or "to congregate." Thus, it can literally mean "one who assembles" or "one congregating." The gender of the participle is actually feminine, but that does not automatically refer to a female. The form may imply a person of rank or simply a collective group of some position.

Compare another participle with a feminine ending, *yoshevet*, meaning "O inhabitant (of Lachish)" or some other locale in Micah 1:11, 12, 13, 15 or Isa 12:6. Or consider *mevaseret* meaning "(O Zion), bearer of good news" in Isa 40:9. Either form allows for either an individual or as a collective reference. *Kohelet* is an individual in chapter one but may have a broader collective sense in connection with "words of the wise" (plural) in 12:11. The KJV along with the LSB translate it as "Preacher" and that may not be far from the original meaning. In other words, this is one who leads a congregation and teaches it, as *Kohelet* does in this book.

## The Author

The traditional view from both Jewish and Christian circles is that the author was Solomon, although his name does not appear in the book. The place to begin is 1:1: "The words of the Preacher (*Kohelet*), the son of David, king in Jerusalem." Although it is possible that the Biblical expression "son of" can mean "descendant of," without a context to impart that special "descendant of" usage, the most natural reading would be that this refers to Solomon, the son of David.

Is there internal evidence to support Solomonic authorship? First there are references to the author's great wisdom. "I spoke within my heart, saying, 'Behold, I have magnified and increased wisdom more than all who were over Jerusalem before me; and my heart has seen an abundance of wisdom and knowledge'" (1:16). "My wisdom also stood by me" (2:9). Then there is an extended passage describing the great works of the author that fits well with King Solomon (2:4–11). Consider the following selection: "I made my works great: I built houses for myself.... Also I possessed flocks and herds larger than all who preceded me in Jerusalem.... Also, I collected for myself silver and gold and the treasure of kings and provinces. Then I became great and increased more than all who preceded me in Jerusalem." The passage also includes an admission of another Solomonic characteristic. "I provided for myself male and female singers and the pleasures of the sons of men—many concubines." Some have doubted that Solomon could have written the statement about "all in Jerusalem before me," since his father had only taken the city a few decades before. Nevertheless, Solomon could be referring not only to David but also to the previous Jebusite kings over this fortress city of Jebus/Jerusalem. If this is the case, he could also be referring to Melchizedek, an earlier "King of Salem" (Gen 14:18).

Rabbinic tradition is also consistent that the author was Solomon. "It was certainly divinely inspired and that is the reason that the book of Kohelet was added to the canon; as was it this alone that Solomon said?" (*Megillah* 71). And while we may differ about the chronological order of the compositions, the authorship of the book was never doubted by the rabbis. "Solomon wrote the Song with its stress on love, in his youth; Proverbs, with its emphasis upon practical problems, in midlife; and *Kohelet*, with its characteristic pessimism, in old age" (*Shir Hashirim Rabbah*). Early NT authors like Paul recognized that Jews "were entrusted with the oracles of God" (Rom 3:2), so Solomonic authorship has been no problem with believing Christians. The question of where exactly we should locate this book in the life of Solomon is an important one, however, and this question will concern us greatly in the following chapter.

## Estimates of the Book

In skeptical circles, this book has been applauded as expressing the legitimate pessimism and doubts about any "meta-narrative" in the world of philosophy and ethics. Its apparent view about the ultimate meaningless of life is welcomed by postmodern thinkers who despair of ever finding an ultimate meaning to life and truth. Others who speculate about the meaning of the Bible's message but are troubled by *Kohelet*'s apparent pessimism have viewed its inclusion in the biblical canon as a mistake.

But it is the approach to the book by some Evangelical writers that should most concern us. Many a Fundamentalist should be shocked by the following comment in a widely used Bible—as a matter of fact, this is the Bible that fed my soul in the early days of my Christian life: "This is the book of man 'under the sun' reasoning about life. Inspiration sets down accurately what passes, but the conclusions and reasonings are, after all, man's. The 'conclusion' (12:13) is legal, the best that man apart from redemption can do, and does not anticipate the Gospel" (*Scofield Reference Bible*, 696). Later he writes, "Verse 10 is no more a divine revelation concerning the state of the dead than any other conclusion of 'the Preacher' is such a revelation. These reasonings of man apart from divine revelation are set down by inspiration just as the words of Satan are so set down" (702 on 9:10). Or consider the following opinion of a popular Baptist preacher from an earlier generation. "No one can deny that it contains statements at variance with the remainder of Bible teaching and gives its approval to things Christians denounce. Even if we decide that the Book is contradictory and impossible to understand we cannot dispense with it" (Robert Lee, *Outlined Bible*).

Yes, such quotes are shocking, not because they come from liberals and higher critics but because they come from authors who profess to have a "high" view of inspiration. The above views are simply impossible to square with the testimony of the author about his own writing as recorded in 12:9–14. It is best that we quote here at least verses 9–11 and then isolate seven points that show how wrong are the above estimates of the books. They also form the basis of how the entire book should be interpreted. "In addition to being a wise man, the Preacher also taught the people knowledge; and he pondered, searched out, and arranged many proverbs. The Preacher sought to find delightful words and words of truth written uprightly. The words of wise men are like goads, and masters of *these* collections are like well-driven nails; they are given by one Shepherd." Consider the following summary statements of the above passage that express what I call a positive view of the author's purpose that makes the above negative views of the book simply impossible to adopt.

1. ". . . the Preacher also taught the people knowledge; and he pondered, searched out, and arranged many proverbs."
2. "(He) sought to find out words of delight and that which was written was 'upright,' even 'words of truth.'

3. "The words of the wise . . . are given from one Shepherd" (i.e., the Lord; cf. Ps 23:1; 80:1; Isa 40:11)
4. According to verse 12 the works of men are wearying—only the words from one Shepherd are building and encouraging. The ultimate conclusion of verses 12–14 rests on this assertion.
5. The language of verse 10 is so forceful that, if we dare assume the preacher's language is not the language of truth, it suggests a calculated error on his part with an aim to deceive.
6. The false opinions of people like Job's "friends" are emphatically declared erroneous in the last chapter of that book (Job 42:7–8). Nothing is stated in our book, however, that *Kohelet*'s teaching was ever erroneous.
7. On the contrary, 12:8–12 affirms that not only the recording of *Kohelet*'s words were inspired but also his message! We conclude from these verses that they present an internal claim to the inspiration and accuracy of the book that is not reflected in the "negative" views previously cited.

So what can we offer as to what is the purpose that the author of *Kohelet* is trying to accomplish in this book? In light of the above and also in response to the overall references to God in the book, the purpose appears to be two-fold.

First, to show that life is a "vanity of vanities" **without God**. The word "vanity" (*hevel*) appears 71 times in the Old Testament and 36 times in Ecclesiastes. The basic meaning is "wind" or "breath" (cf. Isa 57:13). In the book it refers to the transitory and empty nature of a life not lived with the necessary fear and respect for God and His Word. As a statement it is not meant to stand by itself without its surrounding context and apart from the overall message of the book.

Second, to exhort us to **rejoice in life when it is lived with a divine perspective** (2:24–26; 3:12, 13; 9:7–10; 11:8–10). Many readers who have settled for some commentator's overly pessimistic attitude about the author's purpose may be surprised when they discover that the word "God" (*Elohim*) actually appears 40 times in the book! The command to "fear God" appears seven times! Remember that the Song of Songs only mentions Yahweh once (8:6) and in a poetic way at that! Furthermore, the Book of Esther never mentions the name of the Jewish deity even once, although His hand is quite evident in the events.

My seminary professor, Thomas Taylor, summed up the overall message of the book in these simple but eloquent words. "This is the study of a man lost in himself, confused in values, perplexed by circumstances, and annoyed by the events in life. A man who despite these things finds himself in God and the reality of His love, grace, and forgiveness, Solomon is the man, of course, and is identified as *Cohelet*, the preacher" (*Studies in Ecclesiastes*, 5).

I know that simply citing these references without expounding them will not convince a serious reader. In the pages that follow, I will seek to expound on *Kohelet*'s overall purpose which informs a very specific strategy that also provides the key to open its doors. I will eventually provide the entire English text of the book so readers can see for themselves what I am trying to convey as the book's overall message. To repeat, the purpose of the book is not negative, but positive. How, then, are we to understand the seemingly negative and apparently pessimistic and even naturalistic passages?

## A Reading Strategy

Many commentaries on *Kohelet*/Ecclesiastes are extremely difficult to follow. In my opinion, this difficulty is because they have not offered to the reader a template that can be placed on the book through which the author's many diverting lanes and streets can be followed. We should be careful to remember that simply placing such a template or an outline on a piece of literature may not be the best answer. But if that template is the author's own intended creation, then we can be assured that we are following the author's intent in reading the text that way. Those familiar with hermeneutics will recognize the vastly important role of authorial intent in investigating the meaning of a Biblical book.

While I am convinced that such a key is found at the end of the book, I begin with the author's question that he asks in 8:1: "Who is like the wise man and who knows the interpretation of a matter?" After such a question one should look for examples of puzzling "matters" and their "interpretations." Such matters and interpretations actually do follow in the following chapters. In chapters 8–12 there is a series of seven paradoxical "matters" with each one followed immediately by its respective "interpretation." This introductory "formula" in 8:1 that stresses the problematic "matters" and their interpretations is not the only one of its kind, for there is also a concluding formula in this section, identical in sense but different in form. If the introductory key word alerts us to a difficult matter followed by its interpretation, the concluding key word expresses the sequence more graphically in the book's epilogue. Again, we will discover a key at the back door!

Leading up to this concluding formula, we are told that the "Preacher" (*Kohelet*) set in order many proverbs. The question naturally arises about what order and sequence that the Preacher arranged them. The epilogue itself answers our query with the following solution. The arrangement is a series of "goads" followed by "nails." The definitions of these metaphors that rate as "goads" and then "nails," however, have remained enigmatic to many interpreters. Unfortunately, Hebrew lexicons and Bible encyclopedias usually do not solve the contrastive meanings of these terms, and sometimes even define them as synonyms.

Admittedly, the verse in question can be translated in different ways, but both translations retain the implied contrast between goads and nails. The LSB translates 12:11: "The words of wise men are like goads, and masters of *these* collections are like well-driven nails; they are given by one Shepherd." On the other hand, a Jewish translation of 1917 reads as follows: "The words of the wise are as goads, and as nails well fastened are those composed in collections; they are given from one shepherd." The ESV conveys the text this way: "The words of the wise are like goads, and like nails firmly fixed are the collected sayings; they are given by one Shepherd."

I suggest the following translation, based on the literary structure of the verse: "The words of the wise are like goads and like fastened nails are the collected sayings–they come from one Shepherd."

The structure of the verse is a chiasm:

A   The words of wise are
   B   like goads
       and
   B'  like fastened nails
A'  are the collected sayings

Whichever translation is preferred, the sequence of the goads and nails is retained, and their comparison and contrast are of crucial importance in the interpretation of the *Kohelet*'s teaching in the book. Commentators have interpreted these two items in various ways, such as the goads being disjointed sayings and the nails more connected ones. This approach is often then applied to the canonical proverbs of Solomon also being read in such a way.

There is another way to contrast the difference between the goads and nails that will also cast light on the interpretation of *Kohelet* as a whole, and the interpretation lies completely within the book. The "goad" refers to a problem that drives the reader on through a protracted series of proverbs setting forth the problem. Then the "nail" follows each "goad" and like a nail in a sure place it presents a firm and authoritative solution to the goading problem that has just preceded.

Thus, *Kohelet* offers now a problem as a goad, and then a nail as its sure and masterful solution; then again, another goad-like puzzling section followed by a solution that could be nailed up as an authoritative placard or announcement about the problem. The book then continues, alternating between a goad followed by a nail, from the beginning to the end. Therefore, this approach is an interpretation of *Kohelet* by *Kohelet* and for *Kohelet*. It may appear to be novel, but many writers have observed that there is an alternating pattern of behavioral and philosophic positions portrayed in the book. This approach suggests that the alternating of problems constitutes the very authorial plan of the book!

This alternating plan in the epilogue is not confined to that final section. It explains the view already mentioned in the heart of the work beginning in 8:1: "Who is like the wise man and who knows the interpretation of a matter?" The "interpretation" (the nail) that follows the "matter" (the goad) is usually expressed in briefer terms than the goad.

Further reflection on these two physical images may help to clarify the intent. The ox-goad (*darban*) was a farmer's spear-like wooden stick, perhaps as much as eight feet long, with a metal point on its end, intended to goad the oxen (Judg 3:31; see a NT example in Acts 26:14). On the other hand, the nail (*mashmerah*) was a carpenter's tool, usually made of iron, and used to construct objects as large as gates (1 Chron 22:3; Isa 41:7). A golden one was used for affixing ornamented plates or tablets to the walls and ceiling of the temple (2 Chron 3:9).

What is also important to notice is that *Kohelet* 12:11 declares that these words are given from "one Shepherd." From the context it is hardly possible to offer any other interpretation than that this "Shepherd" is Yahweh. Other OT texts that support this identification are Pss 23:1; 80:1; 95:7; Isa 40:11; and Ezek 34:12.

If the goad represents the viewpoint of the problem and the nail that of the solution or interpretation, is there a similar alternation of standpoints elsewhere in wisdom literature? Yes, there is! In the Book of Job we see the alternation of Job's speeches with those of his friends, while his standpoint receives affirmation in the book's epilogue (42) and his friends' ideas are rejected. There is a similar alternation of viewpoints in Psalm 73. In that psalm the writer complains about a series of goading problems concerning the prosperity of the wicked. These "matters" do not receive any "interpretation" (using the language of *Kohelet* 8:1) until the psalmist went into the sanctuary of God and contemplated the just end of the wicked. In other words, the "nail" in Psalm 73:17-28 follows the "goad" in Psalm 73:2-16.

In the same way, *Kohelet* had his disturbing "matters" and then their satisfying "interpretations." He too respects the sanctuary of Yahweh and accordingly urges his readers, "Guard your steps as you go to the house of God and draw near to listen rather than to offer the sacrifice of fools; for they do not know they are doing evil. Do not be hasty with your mouth or impulsive in your heart to bring up a matter in the presence of God. For God is in heaven but you are on the earth; therefore let your words be few" (5:1–2).

As mentioned in the Preface, I discovered this approach to the book in an article published in 1955 by Martin Wyngaarden, who taught at Calvin Seminary over sixty years ago. The only "commentary" that I have found that follows through on this approach is the out-of-print book by Richard De Haan titled *The Art of Staying off Dead-End Streets*. I summarize De Haan's explanation as follows. The goads that Solomon includes are the recollections and concerns which arise in one who is willing to face things as they are. Their "pokes" are painful and do not in themselves provide answers to our needs, but they often bring to light our sinfulness and helplessness and can thereby get us headed in the right direction. When we are finally driven to faith, they have served their purpose. The nails, which refer to long spikes or tent stakes, are the truths which come from God through special revelation. The goads which prick the mind and conscience are of tremendous value for they can drive us away from ourselves and cause us to lose confidence in our own wisdom. But that is all they can do, because they must be supplemented by the nails of God's wisdom, that special revelation that shows us how to be delivered from the guilt of sin and brought into a relationship of believing and trusting in the one true God (De Haan, 13).

We must be careful to recognize the many "goad" passages when we see them, but *Kohelet* also gave us many "nails" of divine truth. When driven home, these "spikes of truth" give stability to life and bring a peace from God. "The goads demonstrate that life without God is a dead-end street, while the nails of revelation point the way out of that street to life" (DeHaan, 14). It is easy to suggest such a template for reading these ins and outs of the many paths in *Kohelet*, but does the entire text of the book really work out in this neat way? In the following chapter, I will invite the reader to affirm how this approach becomes clear in the minutiae of the book's textual details.

# 6

# Tracing the Goads and Nails

## Reading the Book

In the previous chapter a "reading strategy" for *Kohelet* was proposed. If this approach is valid, it should be evident to a careful reader. The purpose of this chapter is to lay out the full text of the book with an accompanying guide to help the reader walk through its various lanes and alleys. As with the Song of Songs, the entire text of *Kohelet* is included from the *Legacy Standard Bible*. Each of the "Four Discourses" will be preceded by a brief outline of that discourse. The English text of that section will follow with the verses that compose the "nail" in bold type. Then a brief summary of that discourse with a practical application will conclude each section.

Many commentators recognize that the book opens with a brief title (1:1–2), which is then followed by four larger discourses (chapters 1–2; 3–5; 6–7; 8–12); it then concludes with an epilogue (12:9–14).

Opening Title and Theme 1:1–2
First Discourse 1:3–2:26
Second Discourse 3:1–5:20
Third Discourse 6:1–7:29
Fourth discourse 8:1–12:8
Epilogue 12:9–14

## Outline of the First Discourse

A. First Discourse (chapters 1–2)
    1. "**Goad**" (1:2–2:23)
- All is subject to vanity (1:2–11).
- Strivings after earthly wisdom (1:12–18), and selfish pursuits (2:1–23) are vain.

    2. "**Nail**" (2:24–26)
- The man who pleases God has a higher standpoint.
- He gives knowledge and joy.

## Text of the First Discourse
## (please read all of the text)

### Chapter One

*All is Vanity*

1 The words of the Preacher, the son of David, king in Jerusalem.
2 "Vanity of vanities," says the Preacher,
"Vanity of vanities! All is vanity."

3 What advantage does man have in all his labor
In which he labors under the sun?
4 A generation goes and a generation comes,
But the earth stands forever.
5 Also, the sun rises and the sun sets;
And hastening to its place it rises there *again*.
6 Going toward the south,
Then circling toward the north,
The wind goes circling along;
And on its circular courses the wind returns.
7 All the rivers go into the sea,
Yet the sea is not full.
To the place where the rivers go,

There they continually go.
8 All things are wearisome;
Man is not able to speak *of it*.
The eye is not satisfied with seeing,
Nor is the ear filled with hearing.
9 That which has been is that which will be,
And that which has been done is that which will be done.
So there is nothing new under the sun.
10 Is there anything of which one might say,
"See this, it is new"?
Already it has been for ages
Which were before us.
11 There is no remembrance of earlier things;
And also of the later things which will be,
There will be for them no remembrance
Among those who will come later *still*.

## The Vanity of Wisdom

12 I, the Preacher, have been king over Israel in Jerusalem.
13 And I gave my heart to seek and explore by wisdom concerning all that has been done under heaven. *It* is a grievous endeavor *which* God has given to the sons of men with which to occupy *themselves*.
14 I have seen all the works which have been done under the sun, and behold, all is vanity and striving after wind.
15 What is bent cannot be straightened, and what is lacking cannot be counted.
16 I spoke within my heart, saying, "Behold, I have magnified and increased wisdom more than all who were over Jerusalem before me; and my heart has seen an abundance of wisdom and knowledge."
17 And I gave my heart to know wisdom and to know madness and simpleminded folly; I came to know that this also is striving after wind.
18 Because in much wisdom there is much vexation, and *whoever* increases knowledge increases pain.

## Chapter Two

### The Vanity of Pleasure and Possessions

1 I said in my heart, "Come now, I will test you with gladness, so that you shall see good things." And behold, it too was vanity.
2 I said of laughter, "It is madness," and of gladness, "What does it do?"
3 I explored with my heart *how* to stimulate my body with wine—while my heart was guiding *me* wisely—and how to seize simpleminded folly, until I could see where is this good for the sons of men *in* what they do under heaven the few days of their lives.
4 I made my works great: I built houses for myself; I planted vineyards for myself;
5 I made for myself gardens and parks, and I planted in them all kinds of fruit trees;
6 I made for myself pools of water from which to water a forest of growing trees.
7 I bought male and female slaves, and I had homeborn slaves. Also I possessed flocks and herds larger than all who preceded me in Jerusalem.
8 Also, I collected for myself silver and gold and the treasure of kings and provinces. I provided for myself male and female singers and the pleasures of the sons of men—many concubines.
9 Then I became great and increased more than all who preceded me in Jerusalem. My wisdom also stood by me.
10 All that my eyes asked for I did not refuse them. I did not withhold my heart from any gladness, for my heart was glad because of all my labor, and this was my reward for all my labor.
11 Thus I turned to all my works which my hands had done and the labor which I had labored to do, and behold, all was vanity and striving after wind, and there was no advantage under the sun.

### Wisdom Exceeds Folly

12 So I turned to see wisdom, madness, and simpleminded folly. What *will* the man *do* who will come after the king *except* what has already been done?

13 And I saw that there is an advantage in wisdom over simpleminded folly as light has an advantage over darkness.
14 The wise man's eyes are in his head, but the fool walks in darkness. And yet I know that the fate of one becomes the fate of all of them.
15 Then I said in my heart, "As is the fate of the fool, so will my fate be also. Why then have I been extremely wise?" So I said in my heart, "This too is vanity."
16 For there is no remembrance of the wise man along with the fool forever, inasmuch as *in* the coming days all will be forgotten. And how the wise man dies with the fool!
17 So I hated life, for the work which had been done under the sun was grievous to me; because everything is vanity and striving after wind.

## The Vanity of Labor

18 Thus I hated all the fruit of my labor for which I had labored under the sun, for I must leave it to the man who will come after me.
19 And who knows whether he will be a wise man or a *man of* simpleminded folly? Yet he will have power over all the fruit of my labor for which I have labored and for which I have acted wisely under the sun. This too is vanity.
20 Therefore I turned my heart to despair of all my labor for which I had labored under the sun.
21 When there is a man who has labored with wisdom, knowledge, and skill, then he gives his portion to one who has not labored with them. This too is vanity and a great evil.
22 For what does a man get in all his labor and in the striving of his heart with which he labors under the sun?
23 Because all his days his endeavor is painful and vexing; even at night his heart does not lie down. This too is vanity.
**24 There is nothing better for a man *than* to eat and drink and have his soul see good in his labor. This also I have seen that it is from the hand of God.**
**25 For who can eat and who can have enjoyment outside of Him?**

**26 For to a man who is good before Him, He has given wisdom and knowledge and gladness, while to the sinner He has given the endeavor of gathering and collecting so that he may give to one who is good before God. This too is vanity and striving after wind.**

## Comment on the First Discourse

The first discourse (1:2–2:26) presents a goading problem in 1:12–2:23, where it shows that man and nature are subject to vanity in their labors (1:2–11). This discourse then shows that strivings after earthly wisdom (1:12–18) as well as selfish pursuits (2:1–23) under the sun are vain and not satisfying. So thus far this discourse comprises what the epilogue calls a "goad" (12:11). However, at the close of this first discourse Kohelet makes a transition (2:24–26) and points in contrast the higher standpoint of the one who pleases God. To this one a grateful acceptance of the present good is actually a blessing from the hand of God (2:24) who gives him wisdom and knowledge and gladness (2:26). This end of the first discourse constitutes what 8:1 calls an "interpretation" and what the epilogue designates as a "nail."

God bestows wisdom and knowledge on those who trust Him. Thus, an uneducated believer can actually have a better understanding of life than a brilliant scientist who rejects God's will and revelation. He may not grasp all the facts of history, but he can recognize that God is at work in that history, and he can anticipate by faith the future heavens and earth concerning which the scriptures speak. "Sensualism, human achievement, fame and even the highest form of cultural pleasure cannot produce a fraction of the true happiness experienced by the believer who walks with God" (De Haan, 48).

## Outline of Second Discourse

B. Second Discourse (chapters 3–5)
    1. **"Nail"** (3:1–15)
- Life is a gift of God.
- Our activities depend on God's providential times.
- The fear of God leads to the highest good.

2. **"Goad"** (3:16–4:16)
     - Man may live from a lower standpoint (i.e., "under the sun").
     - As long as he saw things this way, he did not favor immortality.
     - cf. 1 Kings 11:5–7 ("a sunworshipper"?)
  3. **"Nail"** (5:1–20)
     - The "house of God" brings home the thought: "the fear of God" (v. 7).
     - The highest good is serving Him in obedience.

## Text of Second Discourse

*Chapter Three*

*A Time for Everything*

1 There is an appointed time for everything. And there is a time for every matter under heaven—
2 A time to give birth and a time to die;
A time to plant and a time to uproot what is planted.
3 A time to kill and a time to heal;
A time to tear down and a time to build up.
4 A time to weep and a time to laugh;
A time to mourn and a time to dance.
5 A time to throw stones and a time to gather stones;
A time to embrace and a time to shun embracing.
6 A time to search and a time to lose;
A time to keep and a time to throw away.
7 A time to tear apart and a time to sew together;
A time to be silent and a time to speak.
8 A time to love and a time to hate;
A time for war and a time for peace.
9 What advantage is there to the worker from that in which he labors?
10 I have seen the endeavor which God has given the sons of men with which to occupy themselves.

## God Set Eternity in the Heart of Man

**11 He has made everything beautiful in its time. He has also set eternity in their heart, yet so that man will not find out the work which God has done from the beginning even to the end.**
**12 I know that there is nothing better for them than to be glad and to do good in one's lifetime;**
**13 moreover, that every man who eats and drinks and sees good in all his labor—it is the gift of God.**
**14 I know that everything God does will be forever; there is nothing to add to it and there is nothing to take from it—God has *so* worked that men should fear Him.**
**15 That which is has been already and that which will be has already been, yet God seeks what is pursued.**
16 Furthermore, I have seen under the sun *that* in the place of justice there is wickedness, and in the place of righteousness there is wickedness.
17 I said in my heart, "God will judge both the righteous man and the wicked man," for a time for every matter and for every work is there.
18 I said in my heart concerning the sons of men, "God is testing them in order for them to see that they are but beasts."
19 For the fate of the sons of men and the fate of beasts is the same fate for *each of* them. As one dies so dies the other, and they all have the same breath. So there is no advantage for man over beast, for all is vanity.
20 All go to the same place. All came from the dust, and all return to the dust.
21 Who knows that the breath of man ascends upward and the breath of the beast descends downward to the earth?
22 I have seen that nothing is better than that man should be glad in his works, for that is his portion. For who will bring him to see what will occur after him?

## Chapter Four

1 Then I looked again at all the acts of oppression which were being

done under the sun. And behold, *I saw* the tears of the oppressed and *that* they had no one to comfort *them*; and on the side of their oppressors was power, but they had no one to comfort *them*.
2 So I lauded the dead who are already dead more than the living who are still living.
3 But better *off* than both of them is the one who never has been, who has never seen the evil work that is done under the sun.
4 I have seen that every labor and every success of the work is *the result of* jealousy between a man and his neighbor. This too is vanity and striving after wind.
5 The fool folds his hands in embrace and consumes his own flesh.
6 One hand full of rest is better than two fists full of labor and striving after wind.
7 Then I looked again at vanity under the sun.
8 There was a certain man without a second man, having neither a son nor a brother, yet there was no end to all his labor. Indeed, his eyes were not satisfied with riches—"And for whom am I laboring and depriving myself of good?" This too is vanity, and it is a grievous endeavor.
9 Two are better than one because they have good wages for their labor.
10 For if either of them falls, the one will lift up his companion. But woe to the one who falls when there is not a second one to lift him up.
11 Furthermore, if two lie down together they keep warm, but how can one be warm *alone*?
12 And if one can overpower him who is alone, two can stand against him. A cord of three *strands* is not quickly torn apart.
13 A poor yet wise lad is better than an old and foolish king who no longer knows *how* to receive warning.
14 For he has come out of prison to become king, even though he was born poor in his kingdom.
15 I have seen all the living who walk about under the sun *go along* with the second lad who stands in place of him.
16 There is no end to all the people, to all who were before them, and even the ones who will come later will not be glad with him, for this too is vanity and striving after wind.

## Chapter Five

### Fear God

1 Guard your steps as you go to the house of God and draw near to listen rather than to offer the sacrifice of fools; for they do not know they are doing evil.
2 Do not be hasty with your mouth or impulsive in your heart to bring up a matter in the presence of God. For God is in heaven but you are on the earth; therefore let your words be few.
3 For the dream comes through abundant endeavor and the voice of a fool through abundant words.
4 When you make a vow to God, do not be late in paying it; for *He takes* no delight in fools. Pay what you vow!
5 It is better that you should not vow than that you should vow and not pay.
6 Do not allow your mouth to cause your flesh to sin, and do not say in the presence of the messenger *of God* that it was a mistake. Why should God be angry on account of your voice and wreak destruction on the work of your hands?
7 For in many dreams and vanities are many words. Rather, fear God.

### The Vanity of Riches

8 If you see oppression of the poor and robbery of justice and righteousness in the province, do not be astonished over the matter; for a lofty one keeps watch over another lofty one, and there are loftier ones over them.
9 But *the* advantage of the land in everything is this—a king *committed* to a cultivated field.
10 He who loves money will not be satisfied with money, nor he who loves abundance *with its* produce. This too is vanity.
11 When good things increase, those who consume them increase. So what is the success to their masters except to look on *with* their eyes?

12 The sleep of the laboring man is sweet, whether he eats little or much; but the satisfaction of the rich man does not allow him to sleep.
13 There is a sickening evil *which* I have seen under the sun: riches being hoarded by their master to his own evil *demise*.
14 And those riches were lost through a bad endeavor; and he became the father of a son, but there was nothing in his hand *for him*.
15 As he had come naked from his mother's womb, so will he return as he came. He will carry nothing from the fruit of his labor that he can bring in his hand.
16 This also is a sickening evil—exactly as a man came, so will he go. So what is the advantage to him who labors for the wind?
17 Also, all his days he eats in darkness with much vexation, and his sickness and anger.
18 Here is what I have seen to be good, which is beautiful: to eat, to drink, and to see good in all one's labor in which he labors under the sun *during* the few days of his life which God has given him; for this is his portion.
19 Furthermore, as for every man to whom God has given riches and wealth, He has also empowered him to eat from them and to take up his portion and be glad in his labor; this is the gift of God.
20 For he will not remember much the days of his life because God allows him to occupy himself with the gladness of his heart.

## Comment on the Second Discourse

The second discourse comprises chapters three to five. It contains three sections: first a "nail," then a "goad," and then again a "nail." The previous discourse ended with a nail and this one continues in the same vein (3:1–15). Thus the message proceeds this time from the higher viewpoint that life is a "gift of God" (3:10, 11, 12, 14), given to the previously mentioned man that pleases God (2:26). The thoughts here are sublime and some of the highest in the book, for instance: "He has made everything beautiful in its time. He has also set eternity in their heart" (3:11). This life is not only to be viewed in light of the present time (3:1–8) but especially in light of the future. "I know that everything God does will be forever; there is nothing to add to it and there is nothing to take from it—God has *so* worked that men should fear Him" (3:14). From this higher perspective, this "nail" shows that all of human activity depends on God's providential times and trials and also upon the way in which He disposes of temporal good, which is to be enjoyed cheerfully, and disposes of the highest good, which is eternal. It is that sphere to which the fear of God leads (3:14–15). Undoubtedly this is one of the firmest "nails" in the entire book.

But after basking in this God-centered perspective, *Kohelet* turns to another goad (3:16–4:16). Mankind may also live on a lower standpoint or perspective which is "under the sun" (3:16), namely the standpoint of the world. This leads to many a doubt and a warped perspective on life. It was an entirely wrong perspective that *Kohelet* "saw under the sun" (3:16; 4:7). As long as he continued to see all things "under the sun" he did not favor immortality (3:16–4:16). This view presupposes a temporary isolation from God.

Not only a possible sun worshiper but sadly a syncretistic Yahweh-worshipper is covered by this goad. This could even be a self-reference to Solomon, as it is also in 1:12. Compare the depths to which he sunk in the narrative of 1 Kings 11:5–7. It seems fairly clear that even the King joined in this evil and polytheistic practice! Such religious practices, ancient or modern, can easily lead to doubts about immortality. It is at least left to be an open question, a goading problem to say the best! Undoubtedly, even though we cannot plumb all its evil depths, this section is what the epilogue would clearly designate as a "goad."

But then again *Kohelet* turns to what could clearly he designated later as a "nail" (5:1–20). He declares that "the house of God" is instrumental in bringing forward the concept of "the fear of God" (5:7). The highest good should be sought in connection with the congregation meeting at that house (5:1), which includes serving Him in obedience to His ordinances. This passage is clearly a "nail" and shows how mankind can "see good in all one's labor in which he labors under the sun *during* the few days of his life which God has given him; for this is his portion" (5:18). Therefore, the expression "under the sun" appears in a good context here in the "nail" of the fifth chapter.

Augustine famously contrasted a life under the sun with a life under the God who made the sun! A modern variation in English could be that God intends life not to be lived under the sun, but rather under the Son.

The peace that people of faith experience when they live in fellowship with God is rich and complete, which the makes it much easier to live one day at a time. The desire for riches and prestige and the methods often required to gain them, carry perils that must not be minimized. True happiness is impossible when greed and ambition dominate. For the person who walks with God, however, happiness is a way of life. "The person who walks in fellowship with God may be penniless, alone in the world, and in poor health, but his joy gives him more true riches and genuine power than the most wealthy and influential monarch in the world" (De Haan, 99).

## Outline of the Third Discourse

C. Third Discourse (chapters 6,7)
1. "**Goad**" (6:1–12)
    - The state of the miser is more evil than he who has not seen the "sun" (6:5).
2. "**Nail**" (7:1–29)
    - The man who has wisdom is better as he "sees the sun" (7:11).
    - This wisdom sees God's work and fears God (7:18).
    - The wise are strong in spite of difficulties (7:19–28).
    - These are due to man's depravity (7:20, 29).

## Text of the Third Discourse

*Chapter Six*

*The Vanity of Life*

1 There is an evil which I have seen under the sun and it is prevalent among men—
2 a man to whom God gives riches and wealth and honor so that his soul lacks nothing of all that he desires; yet God does not empower him to eat from them, for a foreigner eats from them. This is vanity and a sickening evil.
3 If a man becomes the father of one hundred *children* and lives many years, however many the days of his years may be, but his soul is not satisfied with good things, and he does not even have a *proper* burial, *then* I say, "Better the miscarriage than he,
4 for *that* one comes in vanity and goes into darkness; and *that* one's name is covered in darkness.
5 Indeed, *that* one never sees the sun and never knows *anything*; *that* one has more rest than he.
6 Even if the *other* man lives one thousand years twice and does not see good things—do not all go to the same place?"
7 All a man's labor is for his mouth, and yet the soul is not fulfilled.
8 For what advantage does the wise man have over the fool? What *advantage* does the afflicted man have, knowing *how* to walk before the living?
9 What the eyes see is better than what the soul goes after. This too is vanity and striving after wind.
10 Whatever exists has already been named, and it is known what man is; and he cannot dispute with him who is stronger than he is.
11 For there are many words which increase vanity. What *then* is the advantage to a man?
12 For who knows what is good for a man during *his* lifetime, *during* the few days of his vain life? He will make do with them like a shadow. For who can tell a man what will be after him under the sun?

## Chapter Seven

### Wisdom and Folly Contrasted

1 Better is a good name than good oil,
And better is the day of *one's* death than the day of one's birth.
2 Better to go to a house of mourning
Than to go to a house of feasting
Because that is the end of all mankind,
And the living puts *this* in his heart.
3 Better is vexation than laughter,
For when a face is sad a heart may be merry.
4 The heart of the wise is in the house of mourning,
While the heart of fools is in the house of gladness.
5 Better to listen to the rebuke of a wise man
Than for one to listen to the song of fools.
6 For as the *crackling* sound of thorn bushes under a pot,
So is the laughter of the fool;
And this too is vanity.
7 For oppression gives a wise man over to madness,
And a bribe destroys the heart.
8 Better is the end of a matter than its beginning; Better is patience of spirit than haughtiness of spirit.
9 Do not be eager in your spirit to be vexed,
For vexation rests in the bosom of fools.
10 Do not say, "Why is it that the former days were better than these?"
For it is not from wisdom that you ask about this.
11 Wisdom along with an inheritance is good
And an advantage to those who see the sun.
12 For wisdom is a shadow *of protection as* money is a shadow *of protection,*
And the advantage of knowledge is that wisdom preserves the lives of its masters.
13 See the work of God,
For who is able to straighten what He has bent?
14 In the day *when there is* good be of good cheer,

But in the day *when there is* evil see—
God has made the one as well as the other
So that man will not find out anything *that will be* after him.
15 I have seen everything during my days of vanity; there is a righteous man who perishes in his righteousness, and there is a wicked man who prolongs *his life* in his evildoing.
16 Do not be excessively righteous, and do not be overly wise. Why should you make yourself desolate?
17 Do not be excessively wicked, and do not be a simpleminded fool. Why should you die before your time?
18 It is good that you seize one thing and also not let go of the other; for the one who fears God comes forth with both of them.
19 Wisdom strengthens a wise man more than ten *men with* power who are in a city.
20 Indeed, there is not a righteous man on earth who *continually* does good and who never sins.
21 Also, do not give your heart to all words which are spoken, so that you will not hear your slave cursing you.
22 For your heart also knows that you likewise have many times cursed others.
23 I tested all this with wisdom, *and* I said, "I will be wise," but it was far from me.
24 What has been is far away and exceedingly deep. Who can find it?
25 I turned my heart to know, to explore, and to seek wisdom and an explanation, and to know the wickedness of foolishness and the simpleminded folly of madness.
26 And I found more bitter than death the woman whose heart is snares and nets, whose hands are chains. One who is good before God will escape from her, but the sinner will be captured by her.
27 "See, I have found this," says the Preacher, "*adding* one thing to another to find an explanation,
28 which my soul still seeks but has not found. I have found one man out of a thousand, but I have not found a woman among all these.

**29 See, I have found only this, that God made men upright, but they have sought out many devices."**

## Comment on the Third Discourse

The third discourse comprises chapters six and seven. We first encounter a goad" in 6:1–12 and then a "nail" in 7:1–29. The state and the name of the so-called miser is "Mr. Evil-under-the-sun" (6:1) and he is more evil than the one whose "name is covered with darkness" (6:4) and "never sees the sun and never knows *anything*" (6:5). Here the word for "sun" (*shemesh*) is used without the article as in *Bet Shemesh*, the House of Shemesh, the sun god. It is interesting that elsewhere it has the article. The life "under the sun" as it is described here in chapter six is an evil "goad."

Chapter seven, however, offers a contrast to six which is infinitely "better," and that very word appears seven times in 7:1–11! What is better is the "name" and the state of the person whose "wisdom along with an inheritance is good and an advantage to those who see the sun" (7:11). Here seeing the sun is again something good. This wisdom sees the work of God in providence (7:1–14), and it "fears God" (7:18) despite the inconsistencies of this life (7:15–18). It "strengthens a wise man" (7:19) in spite of the difficulties it takes to attain it (7:19–28). The difficulties and the incongruities are due to human depravity since "God made men upright, but they have sought out many devices" (7:29).

> According to the first three chapters of Genesis, God made man in his own image, but through sin he lost the qualities of knowledge, righteousness and holiness (Col 3:10; Eph 4:24). Every philosophical system that man devises becomes a dead-end street. The only way he can enter the pathway that leads to heaven is by acknowledging the failure of his own wisdom and accepting the Gospel of Jesus Christ. (De Haan, 111)

The positive statements of *Kohelet* that lead to the New Testament Gospel certainly make this entire chapter a "nail."

*Outline of the Fourth Discourse*

> D. Fourth Discourse (chs. 8:1–12:8)
> 1. Inquiry: Who is as the wise man? Who knows the interpretation (i.e., "nail") of a thing (i.e., "goad")?
> 2. Then follows 7 "things" (goads) with 7 "interpretations" (nails) from a higher viewpoint.

The fourth and last discourse consists of chapters 8 to 12. The section begins with a question: "Who is like the wise man and who knows the interpretation of a matter?" As mentioned previously, the word "matter" would be the same as chapter twelve's "goad" and the word "interpretation" the same as the "nail." Following this question are seven of these "goads" and "nails." Or in the language of 8:1, there are seven different "matters" followed by seven "interpretations" that form a higher and authoritative perspective. The reader is invited to consult the Biblical text to follow these seven pairs.

## The First Goad and Nail

The first "goad" is the question "Who is the wise man?" in 8:1. The "nail" that answers that question is "A man's wisdom illumines his face and causes his stern face to beam" and "a wise heart knows the proper time and custom" (8:1, 5).

## Text of the First Goad and Nail

*Chapter Eight*

> *Keep the Command of the King*

1 Who is like the wise man and who knows the interpretation of a matter? **A man's wisdom illumines his face and causes his stern face to beam.**
2 I *say,* "Keep the command of the king because of the sworn oath before God.

**3 Do not be in a hurry to go from his presence. Do not stand in an evil matter, for he will do whatever he pleases."
4 Since the word of the king is powerful, who will say to him, "What are you doing?"
5 He who keeps a *royal* command experiences no evil thing, for a wise heart knows the *proper* time and custom.**

## Comment on the First Goad and Nail

*Kohelet* does not use the theological term, Providence, but he conveys it by recognizing that God has established authority for the benefit of His creatures. The king is the temporal ruler who was placed in his position by divine will. Those who honor God will also honor the institutions that God has set up. Proper decorum and respect should be displayed before the king. As part of His providential oversight of His creatures, God has established authority for the order and benefit of society. Those who love Him will accept His providential plans.

Whether these words refer to our obligation to rulers or to the Lord (or both), the effect is the same. Believers under the Old or the New Covenants are to be characterized by respectful obedience to all who have authority, submitting to them as unto the Lord (Rom 13:1–8; 1 Peter 2:13–17).

## The Second Goad and Nail

The second "goad" is expressed by these words: "a man's trouble is multiplied upon him" (8:6). This is followed by a "nail" that can be summarized by this statement: "I know that it will be well for those who fear God, who fear Him openly" (8:12, conveying 9–13).

## Text of the Second Goad and Nail

**8:6 For there is a *proper* time and custom for every matter, though a man's trouble is multiplied upon him.
7 If no one knows what will happen, who can tell him when it will happen?**

8 There is no man who has power to restrain the wind with the wind, and there is none *who has* power over the day of death; and there is no discharge in the time of war, and wickedness will not provide escape to its masters.
9 All this I have seen and given my heart to every work that has been done under the sun wherein a man has power over *another* man to his calamity.
10 So then, I have seen the wicked buried, those who used to go in and out from the holy place, and they are *soon* forgotten in the city where they did thus. This too is vanity.
11 Because the sentence against an evil work is not executed quickly, therefore the hearts of the sons of men among them are given fully to do evil.
**12 Although a sinner does evil a hundred *times* and may prolong his *life*, still I know that it will be well for those who fear God, who fear Him openly.**
**13 But it will not be well for the wicked man, and he will not prolong his days like a shadow, because he does not fear God openly.**

## Comment on the Second Goad and Nail

Later in his book *Kohelet* will summarize this nail by telling us that the duty of man is to fear God and obey Him (12:12). This truth, so often reiterated in the book, is emphasized in this nail. Filling one's soul with good is not some mystery but is a matter of respecting God in all of our ways. "It will not be well" (8:13) for those whose life plans ignore this truth. It may very well shorten their days (8:13), Further comments on *Kohelet*'s views of life after death will be offered in the discussion of the "sixth goad and nail" (11:7–12:7).

## The Third Goad and Nail

The third "goad" is reflected in these words: "there are righteous men to whom it happens according to the works of the wicked" (8:14–15). The "nail" follows promptly with the summary statement: "righteous men and wise men and their service are in the hand of God" (8:16–9:1).

## Text of the Third Goad and Nail

8:14 There is vanity which is done on the earth, that is, there are righteous men to whom it happens according to the works of the wicked. On the other hand, there are wicked men to whom it happens according to the works of the righteous. I say that this too is vanity.
15 So I laud gladness, for there is nothing good for a man under the sun except to eat and to drink and to be merry, and this will join with him in his labor *throughout* the days of his life which God has given him under the sun.
**16 When I gave my heart to know wisdom and to see the endeavor which has been done on the earth (even though one never sees sleep with his eyes day or night),**
**17 and I saw every work of God,** *I concluded* **that man cannot find out the work which has been done under the sun. Even though man should seek laboriously, he will not find** *it* **out; and though the wise man should say, "I know," he cannot find** *it* **out.**

## Chapter Nine

### Mankind is in the Hand of God

**1 For I have given all this to my heart and explain it that righteous men, wise men, and their service are in the hand of God. Man does not know whether** *it will be* **love or hatred; anything may be before him.**

## Comment on the Third Goad and Nail

When *Kohelet* says in 8:15 that he "lauds gladness" (LSB) or "commends mirth" (KJV), he is not slipping into some sort of "Hebraic" Epicurean philosophy. He is simply expressing his appreciation for the things that God has provided which promote this inner "gladness." That is not expressed by silly laughter, but by a truly glad sensation that things are well. You can then stand and smile at your circumstances and be amazed at the amount of enjoyment God truly gives. Your labors can wear you out and leave you in a state of fatigue, but the things that God gives are temporarily refreshing. There is no reason to be gloomy about that! God has given you the days of your life. Reflection on that simple gift should produce what he calls "gladness." A final thought that also should lead to gladness is the simple reminder that we "are in the hand of God" (9:10). Away with the goad of pessimism; that is a nail that brings security and gladness!

## The Fourth Goad and Nail

The fourth "goad" arises from the words: "It is the same for all. There is one fate for the righteous and for the wicked" (9:2–6). But a "nail" soon responds: "Go *then*, eat your bread in gladness and drink your wine with a merry heart; for God has already accepted your works" (9:7).

### *Text of the Fourth Goad and Nail*

9:2 It is the same for all. There is one fate for the righteous and for the wicked; for the good, for the clean and for the unclean; for the man who offers a sacrifice and for the one who does not sacrifice. As the good man is, so is the sinner; as the swearer is, so is the one who is afraid to swear.
3 This is an evil in all that is done under the sun, that there is one fate for all. Furthermore, the hearts of the sons of men are full of evil, and madness is in their hearts throughout their lives. Afterwards they *go* to the dead.
4 For whoever is joined with all the living, there is confidence; surely a live dog is better than a dead lion.
5 For the living know they will die; but the dead do not know anything, nor have they any longer a reward, for the memory of them is forgotten.

6 Indeed their love, their hate, and their zeal have already perished, and they will never again have a portion in all that is done under the sun.
**7 Go *then*, eat your bread in gladness and drink your wine with a merry heart; for God has already accepted your works.
8 Let your clothes be white all the time and let not oil be lacking on your head.
9 See life with the woman whom you love all the days of your vain life, which He has given to you under the sun—all the days of your vanity; for this is your portion in life and in your labor in which you have labored under the sun.**

### Whatever Your Hand Finds to Do

**10 Whatever your hand finds to do, do *it* with *all* your might; for there is no working or explaining or knowledge or wisdom in Sheol where you are going.**

### Comment on the Fourth Goad and Nail

No clearer example of the purposes of both a goad and a nail exists than this section. It begins with that "pessimism" that readers have so often perceived in the book, and it ends with a nail of advice to do all that your hands can find to do. It is not pessimism to add that there will be "no working or wisdom where you are going" (9:10)! We are simply encouraged to rejoice in what God has provided now! These exhortations "to eat with joy" and "live happily with one's wife" indicate the legitimate pleasures of life. It is a command to live joyfully. The Lord has allotted to us this portion of genuine rejoicing. Rejoicing and giving yourself to whatever is set before you means "give it all that you have to give." For many this will end, so for the moment allow joy and pleasure to be part of your life!

### The Fifth Goad and Nail

"Goad" number five reminds us that "the race is not to the swift and the battle is not to the mighty" (9:11–10:20). These words pose some of the greatest goading problems in the book. Nevertheless the "nail" advises us: "Cast your bread on the surface of the waters, for you will find it after many days" (11:1–6).

## Text of the Fifth Goad and Nail

9:11 I again saw under the sun that the race is not to the swift and the battle is not to the mighty, and neither is bread to the wise nor riches to the discerning nor favor to men who know; for time and misfortune overtake them all.
12 Moreover, man does not know his time: like fish seized in an evil net and birds seized in a trap, so the sons of men are ensnared at an evil time when it suddenly falls on them.
13 Also this I came to see as wisdom under the sun, and it was great to me.
14 There was a small city with few men in it, and a great king came to it, surrounded it, and built large siegeworks against it.
15 But there was found in it a poor wise man, and he provided *a way of* escape for the city by his wisdom. Yet no one remembered that poor man.
16 So I said, "Wisdom is better than strength." But the wisdom of the poor man is despised, and his words are not heard.
17 The words of the wise heard in restfulness are *better* than the shouting of a ruler among fools.18 Wisdom is better than weapons of war, but one sinner destroys much good.

## Chapter Ten

### The Folly of a Simple-Minded Fool

1 Dead flies make a perfumer's oil stink, so a little simpleminded folly is weightier than wisdom *and* honor.
2 A wise man's heart *directs him* toward the right, but the foolish man's heart *directs him* toward the left.
3 Even when the simpleminded fool walks along the road, his heart lacks *wisdom*, and he says to all *that* he is a simpleminded fool.

## Tracing the Goads and Nails

4 If the ruler's temper rises against you, do not abandon your position, because calmness causes great offenses to be abandoned.
5 There is an evil I have seen under the sun, like a mistake which goes forth from the one in power—
6 folly is set in many exalted places while rich men sit in humble places.
7 I have seen slaves *riding* on horses and princes walking like slaves on the land.
8 He who digs a pit may fall into it, and a serpent may bite him who breaks through a wall.
9 He who quarries stones may be hurt by them, and he who splits logs may be endangered by them.
10 If the axe is dull and he does not sharpen *its* edge, then he must exert more strength. Wisdom has the advantage of giving success.
11 If the serpent bites before being charmed, there is no advantage for the charmer.
12 Words from the mouth of a wise man are gracious, but the lips of a fool swallow him up;
13 the beginning of the words of his mouth is simpleminded folly, and the end of *what comes from* his mouth is evil madness.
14 Yet the simpleminded fool multiplies words. No man knows what will happen, and who can tell him what will come after him?
15 The labor of a fool *so* wearies him that he does not *even* know how to go to a city.
16 Woe to you, O land, whose king is a young man and whose princes eat in the morning.
17 Blessed are you, O land, whose king is of nobility and whose princes eat at the appropriate time—for might and not for drinking.
18 Through indolence the beams sag, and through slack hands the house leaks.
19 *Men* prepare bread for laughter, and wine makes life glad, and money is the answer to everything.
20 Furthermore, in your bedchamber do not curse a king, and in your sleeping rooms do not curse a rich man, for a bird of the sky will bring the sound and the winged creature will tell the matter.

## Chapter Eleven

### Cast Your Bread on the Waters

1 Cast your bread on the surface of the waters, for you will find it after many days.
2 Divide your portion to seven, or even to eight, for you do not know what calamity may occur on the earth.
3 If the clouds are full, they empty *the* rain upon the earth; and whether a tree falls toward the south or toward the north, wherever the tree falls, there it lies.
4 He who watches the wind will not sow, and he who looks at the clouds will not reap.
5 Just as you do not know the path of the wind and how bones *are formed* in the womb of the pregnant woman, so you do not know the work of God who works all things.
6 Sow your seed in the morning and do not put your hands down in the evening, for you do not know whether morning or evening sowing will succeed, or whether both of them alike will be good.

### Comment on the Fifth Goad and Nail

This is the longest of the seven goad and nail passages in *Kohelet* 8–12. We wrote in the summary: "These words pose some of the greatest goading problems in the book." One writer (De Haan) divides this "fifth goad" into a series of goading problems that pile up one upon another. As you read this long section, it sounds like another largely Solomonic work, the Book of Proverbs. There are proverbs in antithetic parallelism: "A wise man's heart *directs him* toward the right, but the foolish man's heart *directs him* toward the left" (10:2). There are also proverbs in synonymous parallelism: "I have seen slaves *riding* on horses and princes walking like slaves on the land" (10:7). Warnings about folly are prominent: "Folly is set in many exalted places while rich men sit in humble places" (10:6). The futility of folly is evident. Even a little folly is destructive since it is possessed by fools, and while it may be elevated by worldly standards, it remains problematic. We might describe a large aspect of folly as "fun," but when that innocuous "fun" abandons the practical advice of wisdom, it ceases to be "fun" at all and will never bring lasting satisfaction.

Solomon moves into one of his longest nails with the command in 11:1: "Cast your bread on the surface of the waters, for you will find it after many days." In this passage we are reminded that our life is to be conducted on the basis of generosity. The passage conveys the nail of being generous and sharing and eventually you will find the reward of your kindness (11:2–3). Later in the passage (11:9–10) we are reminded to order life in a discerning manner. While God will conduct an accounting someday, for the present we should live rejoicing and following the guidance He has given. Those things that are contrary to rejoicing, we should know to set aside so that the reality of the blessing of youth will become clear.

## The Sixth Goal and Nail

The sixth "goad" declares both the vanity of youth and the pessimism of old age (see 11:7–10). This dark passage, however, is followed by a wise "nail" command: "Remember also your Creator in the days of your youth" and serve Him all the way through to old age when "the spirit will return to God who gave it" (12:1–7).

### Text of the Sixth Goal and Nail

11:7 The light is sweet, and *it is* good for the eyes to see the sun.
8 Indeed, if a man should live many years, let him be glad in them all, and let him remember the days of darkness, for they will be many. Everything that is to come *will be* vanity.
9 Be glad, young man, during your childhood, and let your heart be merry during the days of young manhood. And walk in the ways of your heart and in the sights of your eyes. Yet know that God will bring you to judgment for all these things.
10 So, remove vexation from your heart and put away evil from your flesh because childhood and the prime of life are vanity.

## Chapter Twelve

### Remember Your Creator in Your Youth

**1** Remember also your Creator in the days of your youth, before the evil days happen and the years draw near in which you will say, "I have no delight in them";
**2** before the sun and the light, the moon and the stars are darkened, and clouds return after the rain;
**3** in the day that the watchmen of the house tremble, and valiant men bend down, the grinding ones stand idle because they are few, and those who look through windows grow dark;
**4** and the doors on the street are shut as the sound of the grinding mill is low, and one will arise at the sound of the bird, and all the daughters of song will sing softly.
**5** Furthermore, men are afraid of a high place and of terrors on the road; the almond tree blooms, the grasshopper drags itself along, and the caperberry is ineffective. For man goes to his eternal home, but the mourners go about in the street.
**6** *Remember Him* before the silver cord is snapped and the golden bowl is crushed, the pitcher by the spring is broken and the wheel at the cistern is crushed;
**7** then the dust will return to the earth as it was, and the spirit will return to God who gave it.

### Comment on the Sixth Goad and Nail

It has often been alleged that *Kohelet* sees nothing beyond the grave. Along with a passage like 9:5-7, cultists are some of the first to rush to these texts and confidently assume that they teach what has popularly been called "soul sleep." Death does end the carnal definition of life, but not the spiritual. Both "soul" and "spirit" part the body at death. Our spirit differs from that of a beast (3:21) in that it ascends rather than descends and after death is responsible to give an account to Him (8:12-15; 12:14). While he does not offer a full definition of life after death, *Kohelet* tells us enough to know that he believes in it! A detailed description of that afterlife is simply lacking, but perhaps that is why we can read with rejoicing in the New Testament that Jesus "has brought life and immortality to light through the Gospel" (2 Tim 1:10).

> Solomon's portrayal of old age is admittedly very dismal. Many people die before these evidences of physical breakdown become noticeable. Yet this is an accurate picture of what happens when one reaches an advanced age, and the Preacher has accomplished his purpose in warning young people to serve God while they possess strength and vitality. (De Haan, 152)

## The Seventh Goad and Nail and Epilogue

The seventh "goad" is "vanity of vanities—what is the order?" (12:8). The "nail" follows immediately; the order is goads then nails—"Fear God is the summary" (12:9–14).

### Text of the Seventh Goad and Nail and Epilogue

*Fear God and Keep His Commandments*

8 "Vanity of vanities," says the Preacher, "all is vanity!"
**9 In addition to being a wise man, the Preacher also taught the people knowledge; and he pondered, searched out, and arranged many proverbs.**
**10 The Preacher sought to find delightful words and words of truth written uprightly.**
**11 The words of wise men are like goads, and masters of these collections are like well-driven nails; they are given by one Shepherd.**
12 But in addition to this, my son, be warned: the making of many books is endless, and much devotion to books is wearying to the flesh.
**13 The end of the matter, all that has been heard: fear God and keep His commandments, because this is the end of the matter for all mankind.**

**14 For God will bring every work to judgment, everything which is hidden, whether it is good or evil.**

## Comment on the Seventh Goad and Nail and Epilogue

Finally we arrive at the seventh and last "goad" in the epilogue of 12:8–12. He owns his own favorite goading proverb, "Vanity of vanities," says the Preacher, "all is vanity!" Then Kohelet tells us that he "set in order" many such proverbs, but the final goad implies the question: In what order did he arrange these proverbs? This is followed by the "interpretation" (the final nail) that the order and sequence (to use a modern phrase) is that of "goads" then "nails." The noun *Kohelet* can allow for an individual reference to Solomon or also a collective reference to wise men: "The words of wise men are like goads, and the collections are like well-driven nails; they are given by one Shepherd" (12:10). His final "poke" is what has been called the student's favorite verse: "much devotion to books is wearying to the flesh."

The grand finale, namely the finest "nail" of all, is not humorous, however, but sober as it expresses an appropriate and earnest closing that embodies the heart of Old Testament faith. "Fear God and keep His commandments, because this is *the end of the matter for* all mankind" (12:13–14). Contrary to what Scofield wrote (mentioned above), this command is not "legalistic." Obedience is the first step in effective belief, whereas legalism is an adherence to truth without the heart of truth. It is God's NT commandment also that we believe in His Son (1 John 3:23–24), and when that obedience is given, eternal life is the reward.

> Many textual authorities prefer the translation of 12:13 as "This is the whole man." In other words, man reaches the full ideal for which God created him when he lives in the fear of God and keeps His commandments. The Lord made man that he might glorify Him and enjoy Him forever. Man fulfills that purpose when he is right with God. (De Haan, 154)

The final message of this book is that God alone can put the pieces of life together into a meaningful whole. No statement elsewhere in the book can be interpreted as a final conclusion if it contradicts this statement at the end of the book.

## *Kohelet* and God

My seminary professor, Tom Taylor, asks two questions about this ultimate subject. His answers on this ultimately vital subject serve as a summary of *Kohelet* on this theological subject. The reader should note how this theology is not at all abstract but is delivered with powerful practical implications.

1. In a positive way, how much does *Kohelet* know about God?
   - He knows that God is the unchanging force in the universe, omnipotent and omniscient (3:14–15)!
   - He knows that God is just and there is a difference in His dealings with people in accord with their position before Him (2:24–26: 8:12–13).
   - He knows that the "fear" of Yahweh is the one attitude of man that pleases God (5:7; 12:13–14).
   - He knows that God is the true source of our good, and our thanks are owed Him for His gifts.
   - He knows that God will ask for an account of all our doings in due time (12:14).
   - From these declarative propositions, one may deductively conclude, therefore, that God is good, loving, and considerate.

Many of the above reflections are seen in God's dealings with him in 1 Kings and 2 Chronicles. *Kohelet* has talked with God personally, has had his prayers answered openly, and has been given great favor in the work of His kingdom.

2. How then is life to be lived before God?
   - thankfully (2:24)
   - respectfully (5:7)

- cheerfully (9:9)
- considerately (11:1–6)
- honestly (12:14)
- expectantly (12:7)

3. Man fits into the pattern of God's program because:
   - He is a sinner and falls short of God's standard (7:20)
   - God has perfected a way of instruction for him (12:12)
   - Man must come to Him on His terms in agreement with the instruction (5:1–7)

4. Man must ultimately come to this conclusion:
   - God alone makes labor rewarding.
   - God alone is eternal.
   - God alone provides true joy and blessing.
   - God alone is totally just and is the establisher of justice.

Therefore, the truly wise live in the fear of God (*Studies in Ecclesiastes*, 76–77). This book is not the last word on God and His ways. There is more to come—like the New Testament! But this investigation of His goads and nails ought to revivify the idea that those who only see in *Kohelet* the ramblings of "man under the sun" simply have not explored deeply the positive message that the book truly conveys to the reader who works at it and does not overlook the key near its back door!

### *Kohelet* and the Life of Solomon

Previously we have argued that Proverbs fits best in the early part of Solomon's reign while the Song of Songs is located best in his middle years, with Ecclesiastes appearing at the end of his life and reign. What does this last book contribute to the issue of the spiritual condition of the king? We conclude our study of this book with the following general observations on that subject.

*Kohelet* is ascribed to Solomon by both the Jewish and the Christian interpretive traditions. The contents of the book are impossible to interpret if the authorship is divorced from Solomon. Inspiration demands that the book be assigned to him and interpreted in line with the purpose of all inspired Scripture, i.e., "for teaching, for reproof, for correction, for training in righteousness" (2 Tim 3:16). Interpretations of the book vary from the "dialogue of conflict" by early interpreters to the modernist denial by contradictions or even licentiousness. The neglect of the spiritual purpose followed the denial of Solomonic authorship and stresses the pessimistic content. Even some evangelical interpreters have virtually closed the book by so stressing the theme of "man under the sun" to the exclusion of a spiritual message. The approach that holds that Solomon recorded his confession and by it instructed his generation and others is the approach of this commentary. Solomon used *Kohelet* throughout the book as a reference to his office and as an acknowledgment of his own sins.

His consciousness of guilt is shown by the word "vanity" which reveals the emptiness of all pursuits that omit God in government, wealth, or pleasure. He acknowledged the sinful behavior with his many wives by calling it folly and madness. He admitted the depravity of mankind by stating that there is not a just person on earth. He also admitted his guilt of misused wealth (10:18) and oppression of his people (3:16).

His consciousness of God was shown by the many references to *Elohim*, who was to him a personal God who heard his confessions as those also of his father, David. God gave Solomon gifts of prosperity, life, and wealth, but he confessed that apart from God these were still vanity. God's attributes of immutability, holiness, and omniscience taught him about humility before the One who knows humanity's formation and conduct. These truths indicate that Solomon was once again aware of the God he had served in his youth.

His preoccupation with death was that of one who recognized its certainty as well as its consequences. He knew the difference between the deaths of man and animals by teaching that the spirit of man returned to the God who had given it (12:7). He acknowledged his misery in old age by warning young men to remember God before old age arrives. The numerous references to the spirit indicate a knowledge of immortality and the impossibility of being satisfied apart from God. This God had set eternity in the heart of mankind (3:11) and our fullest joy is the happy reunion of the soul with its Creator.

His awareness of judgment revealed that he knew that he and all people will be judged by God for our behavior. The righteous will be rewarded and the wicked punished. He confessed his misuse of God's gifts. Judgment after death will be for every person and involve every secret thing. His readers should recognize that in their context, these confessions of future judgment implied a confession of Solomon's sins and also a belief in the resurrection, despite those goading statements that were always answered by the inclusion of a nail.

Such a consciousness of faith indicates the genuine character of his confession. This confession began with a proper fear of God, a reverential trust evidenced by obedience (12:13). This was then displayed by sincerity in worship and obedience to the Torah as it was heard taught in the house of God. Therefore, his final sacrifices, prayers, and vows were acceptable to God. He also knew that obedience is found in all areas of life before one can be a whole person (implied in 12:13). The king had truly strayed from truth and light, but he returned like the prodigal who confessed that he had sinned against heaven and his father. Therefore, we conclude that by inspiration he delivered to us a blessed book which warns us that all is vanity that is done apart from God. The silence of the Book of Kings about Solomon's repentance is a perplexing issue. Perhaps the historian desired for Solomon himself to communicate his own regret for his deeds!

## *Kohelet* and the New Testament

Many have observed that the book is not cited directly by the writers of the New Testament. However, Paul's statement that we brought nothing into this world and it is certain we will take nothing out (1 Tim 6:7) could be an echo of a verse such as "All go to one place. All are from the dust, and to dust all return" (3:20). Furthermore, it is possible that 7:2 is echoed in Matt 5:3, 4; 5:2 in Matt 6:7; 6:2 in Luke 12:20; 11:5 in John 3:8; 12:14 in 2 Cor 5:10; 5:1 in

1 Tim 3:15; and 5:6 in 1 Cor 11:10. But dogmatism in this regard is to be avoided.

This question raises a prior question, namely, how are we to decide on the presence or the absence of the influence of one book upon another? How do we detect such influence if it is really there? One approach is to look for literary correspondence, in words and phrases, and in idiom. It is in this sense that Bible students tell us that *Kohelet* has left no influence in the New Testament.

There is another way, however, in which OT influence shows itself in the NT apart from a strict quotation. The ideas in one earlier text may be found in a later text without being a direct quotation. The ideas may be alluded to but expressed in different words. Remember that there can be quotations but also allusions.

Perhaps, therefore, it is a writing like the Letter of James, half-brother of Lord Jesus, who comes nearest to *Kohelet* in its tone and teaching. Consider, as just one example, the following section from that book.

> Come now, you who say, "Today or tomorrow we will go to such and such a city, and spend a year there and engage in business and make a profit." Yet you do not know what your life will be like tomorrow. You are a vapor that appears for a little while and then vanishes away. Instead, you ought to say, "If the Lord wills, we will live and also do this or that." But as it is, you boast in your arrogance. All such boasting is evil. Therefore, to one who knows to do *the* right thing and does not do it, to him it is sin. (James 4:13–17)

In this familiar passage, James is not condemning planning or travel or even the making of money. All these activities are legitimate human endeavors. What he is warning about is that life today does not guarantee life tomorrow. The same teaching is found in Jesus' teaching about the man who planned to build better and greater barns to store food in order to fund his retirement, but it was all for nothing when he unexpectedly died (Luke 12:16–21). These are the same themes we find elaborated in *Kohelet*, or as we know it better, Ecclesiastes.

## *Kohelet's* Conclusions

The traditions of history, the content of the book, and the truth of inspiration all relate *Kohelet* to Solomon. Orthodox Jews have been able to find edification in the book and read it during the festival of *Sukkot*. Believing Christians have appreciated it too, while at the same time rejecting those who simply champion human wisdom as the content of the book. Rationalists degrade the book as they also deny Solomonic authorship. Some evangelicals acknowledge Solomon's authorship but question its spiritual value by stressing the expression "the man under the sun," which produces legalistic conclusions. This approach, however, neglects the role of inspiration which demands a larger spiritual purpose. The book, in our opinion, comprises the confession of Solomon after his repentance and thus satisfies this ultimate principle.

The king's admission of guilt and his acknowledgement of God are witnessed by the forty references to *Elohim* as the one personal God who gave him both travail and prosperity, wisdom, life, and wealth, and who displayed the attributes of eternity, holiness, and omniscience. The references to death and judgment are evidence of his affirmation of a future life, while his evidences of faith and obedience indicate the solution to his problem as a genuine renewal of his relationship to God.

Proper reverence for God will be seen in worship and in all the associations of life because every secret thing will be brought into judgment. The prodigal has returned, confessing his sins and warning all from the wisest and wealthiest to the foolish and the poorest that a life without God as the guide is nothing but a vapor, empty of true value or purpose.

## Suggested Commentaries

There are other commentators who take a "positive" view of the book. See the one by my seminary professor, Thomas V. Taylor, *Studies in Ecclesiastes* (Gospel Folio, 2013). An author who sees the structure of the book as embodying "goads" and "nails" is *The Art of Staying Off Dead End Streets* by R.W. DeHaan (Victor Books,

1974). The following article by Martin Wyngaarden of Calvin Seminary effectively argues for the "goads" and "nails" approach to the book's structure: "The Interpretation of Ecclesiastes," *The Calvin Forum* (55): 57–60. The dissertation by my college professor, Fred Afman, "Relationship of Song of Songs and Ecclesiastes to the Life of Solomon" (BJU, 1966), has greatly helped me throughout the writing of this book. He has also related both the book and the Song to Solomon's career in a very effective way, which is the final subject we now turn to at the end.

# 7

# The Preacher and the Song

One of the purposes of this commentary has been to develop a better understanding of Solomon and the writings of Solomon by relating them to his history. The early life of Solomon from his birth through the first half of his reign as king are beyond reproach: he was Jedidiah, the beloved of Yahweh, and he loved Yahweh. This love was evident by his obedience to his father and to his God. His gifts were a proof that he enjoyed the Divine favor. Yahweh's presence in the temple, which had been built according to the Divine plans that David received, indicated His approval of the temple, the people, and most of all, the king.

Solomon's tragic fall, brought on by the many wives that turned his heart to idolatry, raises the question of his eternal destiny. Reflecting on the role of these books in his life shows that no question remains when his writings are related to the history as recorded in Kings. Even at the risk of repetition, the conclusions are as follows:

1. That the Song attributed to Solomon is actually written by Solomon under the inspiration of the Spirit of God and has a spiritual purpose.
2. That the allegorical two-character interpretation neglects the historical relationship to Solomon, declares Solomon to be a type of Christ (although at the time he had sixty wives and 80 concubines), and overlooks the fact that the book is not established as an allegory anywhere in Scripture.
3. That the three-character interpretation agrees with the life of Solomon in his middle years as presented in the historical

books and agrees with the basic principles of a literal historical interpretation.
4. That the three-characters approach can be established by interpretive data and by historical comparisons, so that Solomon's decadence is contrasted with the faith and purity of the Shulamite and the Shepherd.
5. That the triumph of the Shulamite over the temptations from Solomon and the palace exalts human love as a divine gift, which gives dignity and spiritual instruction to human relations in keeping with wisdom literature.
6. That the spiritual purpose of the book is upheld when the Shulamite typifies the believer, the Shepherd typifies Christ, and Solomon typifies the temptations of the world.
7. That the effect of Solomon's experiences was the conviction of his misuse of God's gifts leading to his recording of this experience and a measured but real confession in *Kohelet*.
8. That Solomon wrote *Kohelet* as this acknowledgment and for the purpose of calling his people, who had been led astray by his fall, back to God.
9. That he declares everything that leaves God out as its purpose or end to be vanity.
10. That he declares the whole man is one who fears God and obeys his commandments.
11. That the historical books did not record his conviction and confession because he had already done so in his own writings.
12. In keeping with the pattern in the other Poetic Books (Job, Psalms and Proverbs) the interpretive key to Song of Solomon and *Kohelet* appears in the final chapter of each book.

The Song of Songs reminds us all to cherish love as a sacred gift, whereas *Kohelet* reminds us that everything becomes empty and vain if God's principles are ignored. Because of this exploration of Solomon's thoughts and actions, it is this author's prayer that each reader of these sacred texts will "fear God and keep His commandments," and become a truly whole person.

www.ingramcontent.com/pod-product-compliance
Lightning Source LLC
Chambersburg PA
CBHW050326120526
44592CB00014B/2069